Not every one can
follow a dream but they say that's how much time you
will need to walk the South West coast path and if you
complete the whole trail you will have walked a million
steps and climbed the equivalent of going up and down
Mount Everest three times. The South West coast path
starts at Minehead or Poole and goes around Land's End
and finishes at Poole or Minehead, it goes through
Somerset, Dorset, Devon and Cornwall. The path is a
whopping 630 miles long.

I did not know the path existed when I first
started visiting Cornwall, I accidentally stumbled upon it
one year when I had two weeks holiday to use up. I
packed up my tent myself and my trusty dog Lady and
travelled all the way from Manchester down to Newquay
late one September. I knew the peak season had finished
and I would have no trouble finding a camping spot but
most importantly, that it would be quiet.

I found a site at Crantock quite close to the
loveliest beach I had ever seen. The weather was
gorgeously hot, the sun shone but it was a bit windy. My
friend Marcia had given me a body board she didn't want
and a horrible bright blue and yellow striped wetsuit with
holes in the arse.

I was in my forties then, and as a woman, had
never been camping on my own before, I had been plenty
of times with other people but this was my very first time
alone and it was a little intimidating asking for a pitch
and then knowing a thousand eyes were watching me
trying to put my tent up in a gale force wind. I felt very
self conscious as I wrestled with a tent that was
threatening to turn into a kite. But somehow I managed
it, I was chuffed because they only charged £5 a night so
the whole two weeks would cost only £70.

The following day I thought I'd have a go at body
boarding. It was hot and sunny, I put my swimming cossie
on and we (I mean me and the dog) set off for Crantock

1

beach. The view from the path down to the beach was stunning and I immediately knew I would never have to go abroad again if I wanted a beach holiday. It was all here, sun, sea, sand and I could also take my dog. Plus it was only a few hours drive from home. I thought, I must tell everyone about this beautiful place.

I had never been body boarding before, so as I lazed on the sand and sunbathed, I watched how the others went about it, I noticed their wetsuits were new, black and smart. I also noticed red and yellow flags flying with black and white ones either side of them. It seemed the body boarders did their thing between the red and yellow flags while the real surfers, the ones who stood up, sort of stayed near the black and white flags. OK I thought, this can't be hard, I am going to have a go, so I donned my wetsuit, I was conscious of the bright colours and the holes in the arse but thought, sod it no one knows me. I tied Lady to my bag and hoped nobody was looking as I walked towards the sea. I ignored the lifeguard's laughter as I passed them. The sea looked warm and inviting but I soon found it wasn't warm but bloody freezing especially around the crotch area, after a while I got used to it. I was rubbish at body boarding, it looks easy, all you have to do is catch a wave and you ride it back to the beach. I didn't catch one for ages but found myself really enjoying it, surrounded by younger and older people, all of them laughing out loud enjoying themselves. I thought - this is the life. Then I caught my first wave, the power of it was surprising and I rode it all the way to the beach screaming with joy!

I knew it was time to get back to the dog so I stood up and tried to look like I knew what I was doing, then the next wave hit me and knocked me over so I gave up trying to look cool and waddled, baggy arsed, looking like a wet rag, back to Lady.

Over the next two weeks I got pretty good at boarding, I got a nice tan, my hair turned blonder, Lady and I would jog along the beach, me thinking I looked like Bo Derek in the film 10 but more likely looked like an old demented women trying to get fit.

It was on that first trip to Crantock and from that beach that one day when the sun went behind some clouds and I began to get chilly after my trip into the sea that I walked along the beach with Lady, the tide was halfway out and I saw a cove, one of many on the beach. I had been told about the story of a woman on a horse who got caught by the incoming tide and they were trapped, the horse escaped but she drowned in the cove trapped against the high cliffs by the sea. In this cove I found her memorial. There is a carving of a horse and a ladies face in the rock, it gets covered by the sea every time the tide comes in. Beside the horse and her face is carved a lovely poem which reads:-

Mar not my face but let me be
Secure in this lone cavern by the sea
Let the wild waves around me roar
Kissing my lips forever more

I liked it so much I memorised it and if you ever go there, try to find it, it's not as easy as you think. Just past this cove (now here's a clue to where it is) is a set of steps that are only usable when the tide is out. I walked up these steps and found a path, I carried on walking to dry off and get warm. The path took us high and around a headland and after about 30 minutes it took us to the next beach which was yet another beautiful spot. I now know its called Porth Yoke or Polly Joke to the locals. It is a well painted little beach by all sorts of artists and sometimes horse riders are often seen trotting down to the sea over the sand. I didn't know it at the time but I had just walked my first two miles of the South West Coast Path.

The next day, I took Lady down this path again but this time went the other way towards Newquay. I wanted to see the famous Fistral beach where world class surfers show off their skills and their muscular tanned bodies. The path went across a bridge over a river so we walked over it and soon came into Newquay, we spent a pleasant afternoon on Fistral beach eating ice cream and watching the surfers. Then we walked back to the river only to find the bridge we had used had gone! I know it sounds stupid but I didn't know it was a tidal bridge and that the tide covers it twice a day, I didn't even know about tides at this time or about tidal rivers. So the bridge had gone, I had no map, it was getting late, I had never been here before and I was stood there scratching my head panicking wondering what to do. A woman walking her dog told me I could walk up by the side of the river, cross the road bridge and go down the other side to get back to Crantock but it was four miles. Two hours later, her directions finally got me back to my tent in the dark, I was knackered, I have never felt such relief. Lessons were learnt that day, always have a map and torch and know about tide times, I now know there are two a day DOH!

So I had discovered the South West coast path where you could just arrive at any point of the coast, look out to sea and either go left or right and you would find endless miles of the most beautiful scenic walking anyone could dream of. The combination of a beach holiday when the weather was hot and walking on the coast path when it was cooler suited me down to the ground, I loved it in Cornwall and went there in September year after year. I walked many times on the path but didn't cover many miles because I couldn't walk very far before having to turn around to walk back to the car. I didn't mind doing this because the scenery always looked different walking the other way. I spent endless hours driving, walking and discovering new places.

I did this for many years, some walks were so nice I did them more than once, especially the ones around Newquay and Crantock but only ever in September. I went in August at peak time once - never again - the camp site was heaving, full to the brim with tents, people, screaming kids and barking dogs. The older I get the more peace and quiet I like and when the tent next to mine started spewing out loud rap music, I had to take a trip to Boots the chemist for a pair of earplugs. I was getting more funny looks as well, a woman on her own , people thinking – look at her, Billynomates! My sister always asks me when I do these things on my own "Do you never get lonely" and I reply " I'm alone but I'm not lonely" and its true, I have spent a lot of time on my own, I like my own company and the older I get the quieter I like it. I am not turning into a grumpy old git, I am one already!

I am also a very spoilt grumpy git because I don't have to work. I retired at 45, only because I was lucky enough to sell my house to my then lodger Kevin. It was a bit of a scam really. I sold my house to Kevin who had lodged with me for about 15 years paying me £60 per week rent, (60x52x15 = a lot of money). He was the perfect (kept himself to himself) lodger. I was having a bad time as my beloved dog Lady had developed a brain tumour and was slowly dying, she was having fits every day.

Lady was the dog I fell over after opening my front door one day. She was sat on my door step trying to keep out of the rain. I was always in a rush in those days (but not now) and just rushed past her, got in my car and rushed off to whatever unimportant thing I was up to. Over the weeks and months that passed I noticed her a lot more. She lived in a house full of very young kids and obviously preferred to be out of it, away from them jumping on her and pulling her tail. She was a plain brown and tan Alsation cross, the kind that Manchester Dogs Home has many of and nobody wants because they are not pedigree. I wasn't the only neighbour who noticed how neglected and unloved she was (that's probably a bit unkind to the owners, I'm not sure). I started showing her a little affection, purposely not feeding her but growing to love her even though I tried not to because she wasn't mine. I even used to let her follow me on my walks to the local park and she loved it. She was very unfit then because she had just had a litter of puppies that had all died of parvo. It got to a point where I would purposely go looking for her to go for a walk and if she wasn't out on the street I was disappointed. Over time and after building her a kennel in my back garden which encouraged her even more to look for me and I was always looking out for her. She used to stand on the wall opposite my kitchen window and wait for me to appear, I would see her and feel elated.

For about three years this went on, I was sneaking Lady out off the street, taking her in my car and going for walks, I even took her to my caravan in the Lake District overnight once, her owners never missed her, never knew she was gone, because by this time Lady was sleeping anywhere she could, other than her own home. She slept in my kennel, or even outside next door on a bush she had flattened into a bed.

I had booked a holiday to Truro in Cornwall with my friend Louise and her mum, it was August 3rd 1996, I will never forget that date because the best thing that has ever happened to me happened that day. One of Lady's kids knocked on my door, they were lovely kids and through Lady, I had become friendly with them. I had, for a while, wished Lady was mine but couldn't find the courage to ask the owner to let me have her even though I knew they didn't want her. I was afraid they would turn round and not only say no, but also say they knew what I was up to with her and tell me to stop dog napping their dog. On this day, the eldest girl stood at my door and came out with a short sentence, that even now my reaction surprises me, she said "We are giving Lady away to our neighbour" - I was devastated!! - I just embarrassed myself and ran into my living room and started crying. The poor girl looked so shocked, but to her credit, she ran home, told her mum what had happened and came back minutes later to say her mum said "if I wanted Lady that much I could have her " - I had never felt , in my life, such elation. I went instantly from gut wrenching sadness to being the happiest human being on the planet all in those few words "Mum says you can have Lady", and all because of a dog! What a sad git I am. So from then on, even though I felt guilty and couldn't believe it for months, Lady was mine.

The kids brought her round with a tin of dog meat and Lady was such an intelligent dog, she knew what was going on and couldn't stop her tail from wagging for hours, she went from room to room sniffing her new house, I showed her where she could sleep on an old pink woollen blanket even though I knew she could sleep anywhere she wanted, she was my princess. I am filling up now just writing this!

It was truly one of the best days of my life when Lady became my dog. That night I had to ring my mate Louise to tell her I couldn't go on holiday because I had acquired a dog. Louise and her mum are far from being dog lovers and did not understand why any sane person would get so excited about a mutt. She went ballistic and told me she would never forgive me for cancelling so late, her mum had even cooked a meat pie for us to eat when we arrived at Truro. She just didn't understand and I got angry with her and told her she was ruining the best day of my life, and to this day, now that we have both calmed down, we have a laugh about it all.

For five lovely years me and Lady were inseparable. We went everywhere together, and I mean everywhere, tennis matches, caravan, holidays, even parties, I wouldn't go to parties unless I could take Lady. My sister used to say "It's a bit sad Marie, when your best friend is a dog", but Lady *was* my best friend.

It's hard to say this, but all good things come to an end. I am trying to write this practicably but even after six years it still hurts to write that Lady had to be put down because of an inoperable brain tumour. The back street dog that was so unwanted for the first few years of her life ended up living the life of Riley and knew she was loved.

When she first started fitting, I took Lady to the vets and when they mentioned the word tumour, I got upset, but all the vet did was pat me on the back, offered no cure, only advice to keep a pillow handy when she fell over to fit. For weeks she was having fits and a specialist put her on steroids which made her thirsty and fat, it was either that or euthanasia. I was working at the time, job share in I.T. for the local council. I hated that job and I hated my boss as well. You know how bad it is to witness someone picking their nose and eating it? Well he used to pick his ear wax out and eat it! Dirty bugger! So while all this was going on with Lady, I couldn't face going to work and leaving her on her own and nobody, not least work would ever give you time off for a sick dog. You only get a weeks leave if one of your parents die, you get no sympathy or allowances for sick or dead pets. I phoned in sick because I couldn't cope with the stress of possibly losing my beloved dog. After a few days I needed a sick note, so reluctantly I went to see the doctor. I waited and waited impatiently in his waiting room and by the time I had got in to see him, I was a mess and just fell apart and blurted out, like an old insane crying woman "My dog's dying " I will never forget the shocked look on his face. This made me feel worse, I knew how pathetic I looked, he just turned around and unsympathetically handed me a box of tissues as he asked me "Did I live on my own" which was the worst thing he could have said because it made me even worse, I tried through my sobs to blurt out my predicament about my sad life, my dying dog and my inability to face going to work. He gave me just two weeks sick note, how understanding of him!

Unbeknown to me, a woman of my age starts her menopause, I don't know to this day if the stress of Lady's illness or was it my age that brought it on – I've never had a period since. Was it Lady's illness that brought on the menopause or was it the menopause that made me have an almost mini breakdown? In any case, after two weeks Lady was worse, I had to ask for more sick notes and I still couldn't face work.

My friend Tony came to the rescue and took over sort of, with my agreement, even though I was finding it hard to make decisions at this time. He wrote to my employer and asked for 6 months career break, by this time they were sending what seemed like threatening letters, telling me to get back to work or else. They flatly denied 6 months unpaid leave so I had no choice but to resign. Two weeks later Lady had to be put down.

I can't even write down how bad it is to have to take your beloved dog to be cremated, it was made even worse by a man with punk style red hair who just laughed when we took Lady's body out of the back of Tony's car and into the crematorium. The next day I had to pick up her ashes and pay £35 for the privilege. The experience as anyone who has had their pet put down will know, is beyond awful. I am now over it mostly, the whole thing is in the past now, but I would still like to go back to that crematorium and punch that red haired punk in the face!

The only saving grace at that time was 18 months earlier I had acquired a puppy called Buddy.

So I had left my well paid job, what a knob head, and I now couldn't afford to run my house. Around this time, property prices were at their highest, Kevin, my lodger, wanted to own his own home, I had no income, and interest rates were a heady 5%. So I decided, with Kevin's agreement, to sell him my house, at a much reduced rate and I then became his lodger, the roles were reversed. The plan was, I sold him my house at a low price so he would only have to get a small mortgage, I would live in the house rent and bill free. The money I had left after I paid my mortgage off, which by the way was covered by a useless endowment policy that wouldn't pay it off at maturity anyway, the 'shortfall' as they call it was ten thousand pounds which doesn't sound a lot but my mortgage was only twenty thousand. The opportunity to pay off my mortgage, put the rest in a 5% interest account, then living off the interest was too good to miss. We both even made a will, he leaving the house to me if he died so I wouldn't be homeless, and me leaving everything, including life insurance policies to him which amounted to about the same amount in money terms.

So Lady did me a favour, I would never have taken the plunge into unofficial retirement, its a brave thing to do and I'm not sure I would recommend it, it's a big step and to this day I'm not sure I did the right thing. It's lovely not having to work, I still feel great when I don't have to rise with the alarm, my alarm now is natures alarm clock, it's called my bladder. I can go to bed whatever time I want. It's been nearly six years now that I've not worked, I still haven't got used to it, when I said to Tony, "If I leave work now, I will never be rich" to which he replied "You will never be rich anyway even if you work 'till you retire". That's what finally made my mind up to take the plunge and pack it in. I told everyone I was now retired even though I had no pension (NIKE, No Income, Kids or Earnings). Tony told me to tell people I was a consultant, of what I don't know. I prefer to tell people I am a professional dog walker, which is true because that's all I did at first, walk the dog and spend a lot of time with my slippers. But soon I may have to return to the old grindstone and get off my lazy backside because interest rates are down to zero, I am not earning any interest and I am spending my capital quicker than you can say "where's the money gone?"

CHAPTER 2
Mont Blanc and The Matterhorn

My usual two weeks holiday in Cornwall now had no time restrictions, I was jobless and could spend as much time down there as I wanted, which is what I did over the next couple of years, sometimes going for six weeks at a time. By 2008 I had walked a lot of the South West coast path but only in bits, I love walking, I loved being able to do it on my own, being independent of anybody and the more I walked, the more I wanted to walk.

You would think I'd had my fill of walking by now because I'd done many long distance walks in the past, the best one was Wainwright's Coast to Coast which I did with Tony when I was 39 turning 40. I wanted to escape a possible entrapment by my three elder sisters and wanted to avoid a SUPRISE! party that they were scheming to set up. So I 'did one' and made sure I was nowhere to be found on my 40ᵗʰ birthday. The only way I knew how to get away to somewhere where no one could find me was on the Coast to Coast walk. They tried their best God Bless 'em to find me and very nearly did, they picked the right village and pub I was in on the night of my 40ᵗʰ but didn't spot me in the restaurant at the back. They drove all the way up to the Lake District with a huge pink cuddly rabbit and a cake then drove back home with it because they hadn't spotted me.

The last day of my 39ᵗʰ year was one of the most proudest days of my life so far, we had set off in torrential rain from Ennerdale on the second day into the Coast to Coast, for some reason we had taken our mountain bikes with us, why? I don't know because we ended up pushing them 95% of the time, it's a walk not a bloody bike ride! The rain continued to pour as we pushed the bikes up out of the valley trying to get to Rosthwaite, up a steep incline. On the way there we came across three young mountain bikers who needed to get to Borrowdale, their map had disintegrated in the rain and they were poorly dressed and close to hypothermia. I took a bearing at the summit as the visibility was down to zero, as I did this, these lads and other Coast to Coast walkers started asking should we all turn back because we were lost. I told them I wasn't lost and if they followed me I would get them on the right track to Borrowdale. The only thing was, I couldn't use my compass as I was pushing a bike, compasses don't work near metal, so someone volunteered to push it while I guided this increasing crowd of people off the tops and down the path in the mist. I felt like the Pied Piper. We got to Rosthwaite safely and I will never forget the look in those lads eyes as they thanked me, it made me feel almost Godly, just like a surgeon who's just saved someone's life, they must get that look all the time. The respect I got from the other Coast to Coast walkers over the next week or so was a giant ego boost, I felt extremely proud of myself.

The longest walk I had completed was the Pennine Way, a 270 mile walk from Edale to Kirk Yetholm but I did this in my youth when I was super fit. I did it with a bloke called Steve. We had been training hard to climb Mont Blanc, the highest mountain in Europe, not only physical training but night time navigation around the local Pennine hills. Really we were training to 'sus' each other out to see if we got on under pressure, which by the way we did. We worked together at the local council offices and had the same hatred of our jobs, so getting out and away from the office was both our reason for enjoying the outdoors.

It was 1995 when we travelled to Chamonix in France to make an attempt on Mont Blanc. We had taken two weeks leave and needed only two good weather days to climb the mountain. I was a bit apprehensive because the year before a friend of mine, a very fit fell runner and a group of his friends, successfully climbed to the top of Mont Blanc only to get caught in a snow storm on the way down, they had all the right equipment but the weather was so bad they had to dig a snow hole to escape the storm. They apparently dug it wrong, instead of digging it deep, they dug a long shallow hole and the guy next to the entrance sadly froze to death.

So here I was a year later, knowing how deadly this mountain could be. Me and Steve were getting climbing fit by ice climbing on the Bosons glacier, where in the 1950's an Air India aeroplane crashed into the top of Mont Blanc. Sixteen years later another one from the same fleet crashed at almost the exact same spot. Over the years the shattered remains have slowly flowed down the glacier to the bottom and were reappearing in the receding ice. As we practised our ice climbing we not only saw bits of aircraft sticking out of the ice but also bits of old coats and clothes and even bits of jaw bones with perfect white teeth still attached! They were obviously the remains of the passengers in the air crash, preserved in the ice for over 30 years. We stopped climbing not out of respect but really because it felt a bit spooky, so we just went back to our flat in Chamonix. Over the years, I had always thought I had seen the jaw bone of one of the passengers, but with the invention of the internet, I have now found out that one of the aircraft had 200 monkeys in it's cargo hold en-route for medical experiments, it may have been part of a monkey jaw I saw, I do hope so, as it still gives me the creeps.

We got some altitude training by climbing Mont Blanc de Tacul, a mountain next to the fabulous midi cable car which we took to gain height onto the Valley Blanch glacier where we intended to camp overnight. When we got out of the cable car, we had to make our way over a knife edge ridge of ice and snow which was a bit hairy, then jump over a wide crevasse before actually reaching the top of the glacier. All made difficult with heavy rucksacks full of camping and climbing stuff, the jump over the crevasse with the heavy sack nearly made me wet myself on landing. I nearly didn't make it because I only have short legs, Steve is 6 foot 4, he just stepped over it.

We put the tent up in the snow and ice at the base of Mont Blanc de Tacul, ready to climb it early next morning then tried to get some sleep. Trying to sleep at that altitude wasn't easy, It felt very claustrophobic in the small two man tent and I couldn't get enough air, normally I can sleep on a clothes line. The next day we climbed 'the tacul', it is a bit more technical than Mont Blanc so it was good practise. We got to the summit and had fantastic views of Mont Maudit with the Mont Blanc Mastiff beyond.

It was all a bit scary for me knowing what had happened to my mate the year before. He suffered frost bite in his hands and feet but recovered so he could still fell race, but couldn't play the piano (that's a joke by the way). He said he had tried to change his sweaty shirt in the snow cave but when he took his jacket off to change it, the shirt instantly froze to his body, so he gave up and quickly put his jacket back on, that's how cold it was in there.

We were well trained up and ready, if not a bit apprehensive on my part to have a go at climbing Mont Blanc. All we needed was a two day weather window. We waited and waited and witnessed the most fabulous thunder storms that sent huge thunder bolts around the top of the mountain, there was no way we could climb until the weather improved. Our two week holiday was coming to an end, we were flying home on Saturday, so the last day for an attempt was Thursday. By Tuesday we were worried we might not get the chance, we did as many climbers do, we went to the tourist office for a local long range weather forecast and luckily for us they predicted Thur/Fri as fine settled weather. So on Thursday we set off up the mountain via the classic Gouter route which involves taking a cable car and a tramway. The rest of the way to the Gouter hut was a bit of a scramble and going past the infamous Grand Couloir where rocks came whistling down at high speed making the weirdest sound, was a bit nerve wrecking. We were carrying our own supplies of food, water and cooking equipment, we had no tent just a goretex bivi bag each, we couldn't afford to sleep in the Gouter Hut, it was full anyway, nor could we afford the extortionate price they charged for bottled water.

On the way up we met a couple from northern England, we chatted to them as we climbed, she had never climbed any mountain before, this was her first one, I thought, she must be mad or very brave. When we reached the hut we dug shallow square holes in the snow outside, big enough to lay our bivi bags in and to stop us sliding down the snow slopes in our sleep when we rolled over. It was a clear starry night but freezing cold. After some horrible dried food we went to sleep, or rather I did as Steve was up all night running to the Thunder Box, a little wooden toilet shed that overhangs the snow cliff where all the climbers' bodily functions go. I refused to go in it because it stunk to high heaven, I just did what most did and went in front of everyone else in a snow hole.

When it was time to get up at 3am it was still dark and bloody freezing. Kitting up was hard enough, made worse because I kept spewing up. I blamed it on the crap dried food but it was more likely the altitude. Steve asked me did I want to abandon our climb and go down, I said no chance I'm going to carry on even if it killed me. I don't remember much of the climb, only that it was an easy slow plod and easy route finding because the entire world and his wife were out that day because of the lovely weather. I could only stomach mars bars and high energy drinks. We just slowly followed a long line of climbers over the glaciated terrain, all were geared up wearing crampons and roped up together in case one fell down a crevasse or fell off the Bosses ridge, the knife edge that is just before the summit. If you fell down one side of this ridge you would end up in France and if you fell down the other side you would end up in Italy. If you did fall off, your partner is supposed to jump down the other side to counter balance you and stop you falling to your death – yeh right!

We made it to the top, the views were stunning, and the clouds were way, way down below us. I have a photo of us both on the summit but only because the couple we met on the way up, kindly took our picture as we had click click clicked all the way up and had ran out of film (this was before digital). They then memorised my name and address at that altitude, and that was a woman who had never climbed anything before, they sent it in the post, the only thing they forgot was my surname so it arrived addressed not to Marie Stamp but Marie Mont Blanc. Amazingly they had remembered my address – good on em – I never got the chance to thank them for that kind gesture, but I have now.

We got down without any trouble apart from Steve, he had forgot his sun glasses and on the way down he nearly went snow blind. The sun is so strong at that high altitude of 15,000ft or five Snowdon's, or half the height of Everest, the sun reflects off the snow making it twice as bright, his eyes hurt for days afterwards. We celebrated at the top of the Tramway de Mont Blanc with a can of coke and at nearly £5 a can, we were so thirsty and drained of energy, we thought bugger it, we've just successfully climbed the highest mountain in Europe, so we both treated ourselves to another. When we got back to our flat we were knackered, I had the longest soak in the bath and later we both went out and got drunk. It was, to date, my greatest achievement, no, not getting drunk - climbing Mont Blanc.

Back at work on Monday, our first lunchtime was filled with talk of our climb, but that soon turned to talk of our next adventure. We still had two weeks holidays left, we were very fit, we didn't want to let it all go to waste, so there and then we decided to walk the Pennine Way. Earlier that year I had climbed all five of the highest mountains in Great Britain, Snafell on the Isle of Man, Carrauntoohil in Ireland, Snowdon in Wales, Scafell in England and the highest, Ben Nevis in Scotland. So when we talked about walking the Pennine Way, I thought, what a year that would be, all the highest mountains, Mont Blanc and then the Pennine Way, all in one year, that would be fantastic.

That was in 1995, it's now 2010 and I am writing this all down in my caravan, it is late October, it's cold and raining outside. I have been sat on my backside writing for eight hours now, which is not like me, I am usually up and active doing stuff. Buddy my brown collie cross, who is now 7 years old, is used to loads of walks, he is now making noises I have never heard him make before! I think if he could speak, he would be saying "Put that bloody pen down and get my lead on you lazy layabout". He's not used to this, we're normally up and out for walkies by 1pm at the latest, but today I am making excuses for not doing anything energetic, excuses like - it's too wet, it's too cold or it's too late - well today it's too cold and if I keep writing like this it'll be too late - sorry Buddy!

So in September 1995, me and Steve walked the 270 mile long Pennine Way, just like that! It took just thirteen and a half days. We left one car at Edale in Derbyshire and one at Kirk Yetholme in Scotland. We set off from Edale not with tents but bivi bags and Steve's black and white collie dog Megan. The first night, as we approached Crowden, it began to rain heavily so we couldn't bivi. We asked the warden at Crowden Youth Hostel could we sleep in one of the dorms and leave the dog in one of the outbuilding, he agreed. We sneaked the dog in later, no harm was done and nobody knew any different but it was a bit naughty.

When you back pack on any long distance walk, you try to make the pack you have to carry as light as possible. On the walk, to lighten the load, we had decided not to take food but some new carbohydrate powder that had come onto the market. You add water to it and drink it instead of eating meals. Next day, half way through the afternoon as we walked over Bleaklow, we began to run out of energy and we got really hungry no matter how much of this stuff we drank. By the time we reached the White House pub in Rochdale, we were nearly fainting with hunger so we ordered a taxi to Steve's house in Heywood where we bought a big fat chicken curry and stuffed ourselves with food. We threw the powdered crap in the bin and next day filled our packs with proper real back packers grub like bread and cheese, packet's of crisps, chocolate and cans of coke. We got a taxi back to yesterdays finish point at the White House

17

and on we walked past Hardcastle Craggs and ended up at the end of the day at the ruins at Whitens near Howarth. I remember it well because we slept in our bivi bags in the lean to that walkers use to shelter from the weather. It had two benches inside on which we slept, the dog slept on the floor. Just as I was turning over, trying to get comfy in my sleeping bag, I heard a woman screaming loudly at the top of her voice. I sat up frightened and asked Steve had he heard it, he said he hadn't, I must have imagined it – but I had heard it, I was convinced it was Kathy screaming for Heathcliff ! I have thought all these years that it was her ghost screaming, but recently, when I told this story to someone, they spoilt my memory of it by telling me that it was probably the sound of a rabbit being caught by a fox, apparently they sound like a woman screaming just as the fox kills them – how lovely!

After Whitens, the memory of the rest of the Pennine Way becomes an exhausted blur, I remember getting to Hawes the next night and booking into a B & B that allowed dogs to stay. I remember the comfort of a soft bed and clean sheets and giving Steve's dog Megan the sausage from my huge full English breakfast. All the creature comforts of home like the joys of running water, flushing toilets and television and that was after only one night roughing it. How we managed with no tent I don't know because the weather wasn't that good, especially the last two days.   We had planned to sleep in the refuge hut in the Cheviot hills between Byrness and Kirk Yetholm on our last night but when we got there, this smelly man who bragged that he hadn't had a wash at any time whilst he walked the Pennine Way, was in this hut. All his smelly gear was laid all around the hut drying out. The hut stank, it had been raining all day none stop, there was no way we could sleep there so we carried on the rest of the way to the end, a total of 27 miles in one day, the longest days walk I had ever done. It doesn't sound much but we were carrying heavy back packs. We got to the pub in Kirk Yetholm where a few fellow Pennine Wayers, who we had met along the way were all sat celebrating finishing one of the most famous long distance walks in

England. We arrived too late for food so we celebrated with a pint and a packet of peanuts, what an anticlimax! We got in the car we had left there two weeks earlier and I attempted to drive south back towards Manchester, I only lasted an hour, I couldn't keep my eyes open, I was knackered and was threatening to fall asleep at the wheel so Steve took over and I don't know how he did it as we were both equally knackered, but he got us home safely while I was fast asleep snoring my head off in the passenger seat!

Next day after a lovely lie in on Steve's spare bed, we drove back to Edale to pick up the other car and a certificate from the pub. It stated we had walked the Pennine Way! Another fine achievement - even though I say it myself.

I have writers cramp now! I'm still in my caravan in the Lake District, it's only a small white touring caravan, nothing fancy, just big enough for Buddy and I to be cosy. It has a fire, lighting, a toilet, sink, a cooker and an oven, my sister says its like being in a dolls house. Its my bolt hole, somewhere to just chill out or to go walking or cycling, it's near a beach and not too far away from my favourite place in the world, The Lake District with all it's beautiful mountains and lakes. This year there was a drought here and most of the lakes dried up especially the ones that supplied Manchester with it's drinking water where they put a hose pipe ban on as usual and because the lakes disappeared, everyone was calling it 'The District'.

The year after we climbed Mont Blanc, me and Steve got really cocky and decided to have a go at climbing the Matterhorn. It is known as the greasy pole of Europe because so many people climb it every year. There are numerous Matterhorn guides that will guide you up it for a large fee. We thought we could do it ourselves. In 1996 we set off for Zermatt, a traffic free village at the base of the Matterhorn in Switzerland. The journey from Geneva airport to Zermatt was lovely in itself, the train took us around Lake Geneva and then we had to catch another little train from Gorenergarat which had wonderful views. All this was included in a package holiday with Inghams along with an apartment right next to the cable car that took us up to the base of the Matterhorn. It wasn't a cheap holiday. To pay for it, we had both worked through the winter doing extra jobs, Steve worked at night washing dishes at a local restaurant, I worked at weekends for Barclay's bank replenishing ATM's with wads of money.

We arrived in Zermatt for a two week holiday with all our climbing gear. We did the usual altitude training by climbing the Breithorn and did a reconnaissance to the very start of the climb just past the Hornley Hut. We couldn't afford to stay in this hut so with a good two day weather forecast, we bivvied outside it ready to set off early next morning to climb the Hornley Ridge. There were crowds of other climbers, some with guides, some without, most of them stayed in the luxury of the hut. We had done all the planning, all the training and we were very fit.

We got in our bivvi bags at around 9pm when it went dark, the sky soon turned black, there was no light pollution so the stars were bright, the milky way appeared and shooting stars shot across the sky. In the very far distance, towards Italy, we could see thunder and lightning coming from storm clouds, we could just about hear it, it added to my apprehension I had about the climb. It didn't stop us sleeping though, we were so warm and cosy we slept through the 3am alarm and instead of setting off at 3.30am like everyone else, we overslept and didn't wake up until 6am when it got light. We saw to our horror, a line of climbers already well on their way up the Hornley Ridge. We set off in a hurry trying to catch them up which meant we had to do our own route finding. We went wrong almost straight away and wasted more time backtracking. We went wrong several more times, I was leading at one point and found myself climbing what seemed like the north face. Hanging on by my fingernails trying to find the correct route was very scary, how I didn't fall off I don't know, if I had fallen off I would have pulled Steve with me as we were both tied together by a climbing rope. It reminded me of the incident when a couple had successfully climbed to the top of the Matterhorn and were on their way down, they stopped for a rest, still tied together, one took a photo of the other and while they did this, one of their rucksacks fell from the ridge they were on, one of them went to grab it and fell off, pulling the other one after him to their deaths.

By the time we had climbed to the Solvay Hut at 1200ft, we came up against hordes of climbers coming down after successfully reaching the summit. One of the guides told us in no uncertain terms not to continue as we would be in the way of the other descending climbers and guides. We looked up the ridge and saw a long line of climbers coming down the narrow ridge and knew he was right, the summit looked so near but it would have been a nightmare getting past them. So we had no choice but to turn back. After a few scary abseils, we got back down to our bivvi bags then back to our apartment. All that planning, effort and expense and we had failed! It was too late in the holiday to have another go and attempting it had scared me to death anyway, so much so, it put me off climbing for years.

CHAPTER 3
She Won't Get Far, Her Bag's Too Heavy

In 2009 I was once again on my way to do some walking on the South West Coast Path, this time I didn't go to Cornwall. I had acquired, some years earlier, a set of four National Trail Guides that covered the whole 630 miles with strip maps. The first book covers Minehead to Padstow 166 miles, so instead of going to Crantock, for the first time in six years, I headed for Minehead where I camped at a site at Porlock, a lovely little village about eight miles away from the start of the path at Minehead.

Next day I drove to the very start of the walk, where stands a sculpture made of metal, it's a pair of hands holding a giant map. Buddy and I had our picture taken. I stood there and wondered would I ever get the chance to set off from this point one day and just walk and not stop. The seed was planted, I wanted to do a whole section not just a days walk but weeks on end staying overnight somewhere different every time. But this wasn't that time. All I did was the usual day walks from the car and back wishing that I could just carry on in the same direction. I came across a few people doing long sections and I was so jealous. I wished it was me. I drove further along the coast camping at Combe Martin and walking from there, then on to Bude and more walking but it wasn't continuous walking. Then I headed for my usual holiday at Crantock, I spent a couple of weeks messing around on the beach and walking until I persuaded Tony to join me at a camp site in St Buryan near Land's End. He travelled down in his giant motor home and we based ourselves there for a few weeks. This time we had his motor home and my car from which me, Tony and Buddy visited places like the beach next to Sennen Cove which is great for body boarding and also allows dogs. This is one of my favourite beaches, another is Logan Beach near the lovely Porth Curno and the Minach Theatre.

I asked Tony (but didn't think he'd say yes) would he mind looking after Buddy while I walked from

Penzance to Lizard on my own on a two day walk. He surprisingly said "yes" and so he dropped me off at Praa sands with a back up plan that if I couldn't find somewhere to stay overnight I should ring him and he would come and get me and take me back to the motor home. Off I went down the South West Coast Path in lovely weather and carrying a light overnight rucksack with two days worth of sandwiches in it. It was fantastic, just me on my own, walking, knowing I would either find a B & B at Mullen Cove or if not, Tony would come and get me. I had never back packed over night on my own before, it was a revelation, I was loving it and when I got to Mullen Cove and easily found a B & B, I wanted to find out if I would feel daft staying there on my own but I needn't have worried because I was welcomed by the owner who showed me to my room. When I told him I had walked about 10 miles of the South West Coast Path and was tired, he knew all I wanted to do was have a shower and put my feet up. He told me the time for breakfast and left me to it. This was easy, I could do it on my own, I was tired and I was loving all the comforts of a B & B and I felt at home. I fed myself on fish & chips. Later, I phoned my sister to tell her what I was up to because I knew this was the start of something new, a new independent me. I could do all these things on my own, I know on this occasion Tony was there if it all went pear shaped. All the back packing I'd done before was with someone else, usually a bloke ,but never had I had the guts to try it by myself.

The next day, after a lovely breakfast, where I had to sit on my own at the breakfast table but surprisingly didn't feel self concious, I felt like Shirley Valentine in the film of the same name, I set off for Lizard the most southerly point in Britain. I got the same feelings of euphoria again, I was loving it, I wanted more, it was only about 8 miles. When Tony picked me up at the Lizard lighthouse, which I noted for future reference, had a lovely youth hostel nearby, I thanked him and asked him, after a few days rest, would he do the same and drop me off on the other side of the Lizard Peninsula near

Helford then pick me up two days later at Lizard again. He again agreed and a couple of days later I was walking from Gillian to Coverack youth hostel with the same back up plan as before. I loved the walking on my own, the independence, and the freedom of going from one place to the next and staying overnight. I'd stayed in many youth hostels on my travels in the past but again, never on my own, which is a good thing really because sometimes you can meet the weirdest of people in them. If you think you meet weird people on on-line dating sites, youth hostels take the biscuit, neither have I ever meet a 'youth' in a youth hostel, they are usually full of 'older' people, usually wearing desert wellies (sandals for those who don't know what a desert wellie is) and usually with socks underneath and beards and that's just the women. In fact I was so confident and cocky when I reached Coverack Youth Hostel, I ordered dinner there and sat at the biggest of bay windows with a beautiful view of a lovely beach and the sea beyond with sail boats and ships passing slowly by, that Shirley Valentine feeling again. I thought I looked cool but probably looked like a sad old woman eating on her own, in fact I had become one of those weird people but I didn't care, I had acquired a confidence I didn't know I had, I was on a mission, I was practising for something but I wasn't sure what yet.

I walked the 8 miles towards Lizard where Tony met me. We watched the seals as we shared a pot of tea at the cafe overlooking Lizard Point. I told him that now I'd experienced four days of continuous walking on the South West Coast Path, which I'd only dreamed about, I could die happy, he said he was happy to help (me walk, not die I hope!). Like some hungry monster, I had caught the bug, I secretly wanted more. I promised myself, now I'd practised being sort of independent, I would do more of this, some nomadic beast had been awakened in me, I had wanderlust.

Over the winter of 2009/2010 I subconsciously started planning my September trip down south, I knew if I was to do a large section of the South West Coast Path, I couldn't afford to stay in expensive B & B's or youth hostels; I would have to camp. The equipment you need for backpacking is quite important, firstly it has to be light weight and secondly it has to be reliable. Over the years I had acquired most of my kit but some of it was now old, knackered, out of date and bloody heavy. I didn't purposely attempt to get fit for a long distance walk, I just carried on as usual, walking with Buddy, going to the gym now and again and swimming in my favourite outdoor heated swimming pool at The Lancashire Health and Racket Club at Bowlee in Middleton (is that enough advertisement for a free membership?). Then in the spring when the tennis season started, I played some great matches on their fine indoor and outdoor tennis courts (come on, give us a freebie!). Soon spring turned to summer, I started buying new kit, a new rucksack which I filled with what I thought I might need for a long distance walk and had a trial run on the Cumbrian Way which I had already walked with Tony in 1999. On that occasion I found the 70 mile walk quite easy, we must have been fit because we even walked up some mountains as we went along; Coniston Old Man, Bowfell and the like. Tony struggled though near the end, his bag was heavy and he ended up having physiotherapy on the balls of his feet for weeks after and he has flatly refused to do any long distance walks ever since. This time I was on my own, I didn't take my dog Buddy, I was only going to walk from Ulverston to the Langdale Valley via Coniston over three days with just one nights wild camp at Beacon Tarn and one at Coniston camp site, it should be a piece of cake! I packed my new shiny rucksack which weighed 5lbs before anything was in it, when full, it weighed a ton. It was far too heavy and when Kevin couldn't pick it up, I knew I had far too much stuff in it but set off anyway.

I thought I was doing OK until a walker rushed past me, he told me he too was walking the Cumbrian Way, all of it! His bag looked small and light even though he was camping; he told me he was also heading for the tarn I was heading for, to sleep the night. I was annoyed, I'd wanted to camp there in the wild on my own, not near some stranger who could be a mad axe man for all I knew. Off he skipped light as a feather and left me behind with my heavy load, walking like I had the world on my shoulders. Two hours after he had arrived at the tarn, I arrived, sweaty and knackered, he looked fresh as a daisy. I was regretting not bringing Buddy as security but that would have meant carrying his dog food to add to my troubles. He offered to help me put up my tent, which for some reason offended me, like when a man opens a door for me, I will never get used to it, I must be some sort of raving feminist or something. I declined his offer because I wanted the practise and satisfaction of putting it up myself, but mostly I didn't want him coming near me. we were, after all, in the middle of nowhere (my sister's going to kill me when she reads this). So this was my very first wild camp on my own, apart from this man, who turned out to be very nice, he was just doing his own thing and I had no right to suspect him of anything it was just my imagination running wild. He set off early next day before I even surfaced, I didn't hear him pack up. I slowly and lazily woke up, taking my time, enjoying the beautiful view from my tent of the tarn and the Lake District mountains, the peace and quiet was something else, I didn't want to leave, the sky was blue with wall to wall sunshine.

I reluctantly packed up my kit which took ages, I set off even slower than yesterday because yesterday I was relatively fresh, and today I was stiff as a board. By the time I had reached Coniston camp site, my old injury from walking the Dales Way started playing up. While walking the Dales way in 2001, I developed shin splints, instead of giving up and going home I stubbornly carried on and made them worse. It took months and lots of physio to get rid of them and sometimes they reappear. Carrying this heavy bag had made them resurface so I did what I should have done on the Dales Way, something that is against my nature - I gave up and went home! The new heavy rucksack was sent back to the shop, I got my money back which I put towards a very expensive light weight one; OK I will tell you how much it cost, it was £100 which is a lot of money for someone with no income.

I didn't know this at the time but Kevin had met two of my friends and told them what I was up to. They all had a laugh at my expense at me trying to get back packing fit and they both laughed when he said "She won't get far her bag's too heavy" - OK on this occasion he was right but when my mate told me of this conversation and how funny they thought it was, I was secretly determined to prove to them I could get far and I could manage on my own, it was like a red rag to a bull.

The new rucksack was just big enough for my tent and most of my kit and I mean most because I had no intention of taking as much next time, I would stick to the bare essentials. It was made by an American company, I don't know if I am allowed to say the name but I got a matching black base ball cap with gold lettering on the front that said 'GOLITE', which was exactly what I intended to do. I also knew that if I was to walk for more than a couple of weeks I would have to take Buddy with me. In the past, when I have gone on holiday, Tony kindly minds Buddy during the week and Kevin has him at weekends, which is a great arrangement as Buddy never has to go into kennels. But for any holiday longer than two weeks, it would be a bit cheeky of me to ask Tony to have Buddy for so long; I knew I would have to take the dog and carry his stuff as well. I wanted to take him anyway while he was still relatively young and he would give me some security if I had to wild camp. He had his own roll up bed, a light towel and poo bags, these didn't weigh much, it was his food that I was worried about. Tinned dog food weighs a ton so that was out of the question. He has been brought up on dried food and when I saw some dog packs on Ebay I bid a bargain amount of £8 and got them. He is used to wearing a raincoat, yes I know it sounds silly but we do go out in all weathers, we are out every day and I've done so much outdoor pursuits in the freezing cold; freezing cold wet days are the worst, that's why he wears a coat and my face is like a slapped arse, my cheeks are so reddened by cold weather, someone told me the other day "You look like a farmers wife" - Is that a compliment? I don't know. So Buddy didn't mind wearing these green panniers, one on each side, he looked quite cute really. I put them on empty at first, he seemed very proud to be wearing them. Gradually I started putting a bit of dried food in so he would get used to wearing them on his back. We would go for a walk where no one could see us as I also wanted to test out my two new walking sticks. I was not used to walking with two sticks, I felt a right plonker. They are supposed to take 20% of the weight off you and your legs especially your old knees, that is the theory anyway, it does take practise and after I got into a rhythm it was like having four legs just like Buddy. We must have looked a right sight me with two sticks walking like a marching tin soldier and Buddy with his back packs on.

So after a few more tennis matches to play and with my shin splints strapped up tightly it was now early August. I was trying to think of anything that might stop me having a longer holiday than usual, things like bills, car tax, pet insurance things like that. I made sure there was loads of money in my current account (£2500) and filled my purse with £500 in light weight £50 notes. My sister always cuts my hair, it saves me a fortune in hairdresser fees, I asked her to cut it extra short.

I was slowly building up to the day I could get away and drive down to Minehead. After a celebratory end of season curry with my tennis mates, one of them, Dave, asked me all about my plans for my holiday. I told him I was just going for this walk, setting off, me and Buddy with all my gear on my back to see how far I would get, "Padstow", I told him, would be great, Land's End, I would be chuffed to bits to reach. He took the mickey out of me and said I was being cruel to Buddy who would probably think he was just going for an afternoon stroll not knowing he was going to be walking one of the longest dog walks of his life and not only that, he'd have to carry his own stuff too. After taking the mickey out of me all evening, he started asking serious questions about my kit, accommodation, how much it was all going to cost and how do I recharge my i-pod and mobile phone, stuff like that. He then admitted he was very envious of me and the freedom I had to be able to just set off for weeks on end. It was the same with my elder sister, she's due to retire shortly and as an ex smoker, she's trying to get fit by walking. When she found out what I was going to do she asked would I take her with me next time I was going to do a long distance walk – I was quite chuffed that not everyone thought I was mad to attempt it, it made me feel less of a weirdo.

CHAPTER 4
The Best Plan Is To Have No Plan At All

So the stage was set for Minehead, I had no commitments, I packed my car as usual with all my base camp stuff, like my three man tent, comfy bed, body board and wet suit. With my shin splints still giving me gyp, I thought if I don't get far down the South West Coast Path at least I will know I could just drive to Crantock, sack the walking and sit and sunbathe with my feet up. I also put my four map books in as usual, the only other addition was my new backpack full of my light weight stuff.

With everything ready and nothing to stop me, Buddy and I set off for Minehead with Padstow or maybe Land's End my dream goals. I told Kevin I'd be away no more than the usual six weeks and that if he fancied it, would he like to join us either walking or base camping somewhere so he could see Buddy. He and Buddy are like how Lady and I were – inseparable – Kevin said he would think about it.

Buddy and I arrived at Porlock, about an 8 mile walk from the start of the South West Coast Path and set up camp at one of the camp sites there. I told the owner I wanted to walk from Minehead to Padstow which could take anything between 1 day and two weeks depending on how I got on. I asked him could I leave my car in his field, he agreed but said he would have to charge me £2 per day. So that is what I did, at least I would know the car and all my stuff inside would be safe while I walked.

The next day Buddy and I caught a bus into Minehead, Buddy has never been on a bus, he's used to being in my car and is a good traveller. But he surprised me by howling and crying loudly all the way there, he kept slipping on the polished floor of the bus like a mop, he only shut up when I let him on the soft seat next to me, I don't think the driver was too impressed. We fell out of the bus, me, Buddy and my small daysack and made our way once again to the map in the hands sculpture.

This was it! A lot of planning but not much had gone into this. I put Buddy's empty backpack on him for show and someone kindly took our picture with my phone and said how cute he looked. It's a bit sad when your dog is better looking than you but it's true and his breath smells fresher than mine too! He was getting lots of attention and I was lapping it up like a proud mum. We set off walking towards Porlock and my tent, so we had started, just like that, no fan fares, no nowt, nobody waving us off!

It's a lot easier walking with a light daysack, I knew it would be harder from then on. Next day I packed up my tent and my heavy backpack, parked up my car and said goodbye to the owner. His parting words were – mind where you put your feet – which is exactly what I intended to do with the help of my two anti shock walking sticks. We set off again, this time I had a sack on my back that weighed a ton, - well not really it was around 25lbs or nearly two stone! I wasn't used to the weight and hoped no one could see me as I waddled up the road with my huge sack, looking like I was setting out on a year long trek.

Between Porlock and Lynton there's a 12 mile stretch with hardly any accommodation, well there's one B & B and a pub called the Blue Ball. The day before I left, I rang the pub to ask if they took dogs, which they did and to ask how much for a one night stay. I was shocked to hear it would be £82 including single occupancy. I thought Jesus; this is going to be an expensive trip so I realised there and then I would be camping quite a lot if my bank account was going to last till Padstow.

We didn't make it to Lynton or the Blue Ball pub either. I'd wrongly thought that 12 miles would be easy, I was doing about 20 miles a day average on the Pennine Way but I was young and fit then and it's relatively flat, I remember commenting on how flat it was at the time but I had just climbed Mont Blanc so it would seem flat after that. We, I mean me, because Buddy was fine, only managed a pathetic 8 miles, my bag was so heavy and I was not used to the weight, I felt so unfit. Only 8 miles and I was knackered and couldn't walk another step. I was in the middle of nowhere, I knew where I was on the map but there was no way I could reach Lynton which was about four miles away then walk another couple of miles looking for a camp site. I made my first decision of the walk, I had no choice really; I had to wild camp. I had come prepared after my practise on the Cumbrian Way, I had a water filter which is a kind of pump that makes dirty water into drinking water, I also had emergency food which consisted of a packet of super noodles some cake, powdered custard, some porridge, powdered milk, tea bags and sugar. I was on unknown territory, I had never been here in my life, I was on my own and it was up to me and no one else whether I was going to survive or not. This was it, I was doing what a lot of people would love to do and I was a little scared but I was focused on what I was doing.

The path here was close to the cliff, the views out to sea were stunning, it was a lovely calm warm sunny evening, perfect for a wild camp. I looked around for a flattish spot big enough to pitch my tent, there wasn't much about but about 10 yards away from the path was a nice flat bit. I pitched my tent, found a stream to filter a couple of litres of water, fed Buddy dried food out of his back pack which he had uncomplainingly carried all day. I made some noodles which tasted surprisingly good because I was starving and followed it with delicious cake and custard and a lovely cup of tea which I drank while I watched the sun set over the sea. I felt quite safe, no one could see us and Buddy was my guard dog, well he would have been if he hadn't already sparked out on his roll up bed. I tried to make a phone call to my sister as it was her 60th birthday but had no reception, bugger,I was annoyed with myself for not ringing her earlier when I did have a signal. By the time I had washed up it was getting dark, it was only 7.30pm and all there was to do was either play with my i-pod, one of the few luxuries I had allowed myself or go to sleep. I got into my sleeping bag and fell instantly to sleep and woke up 12 hours later!

I woke up to the sound of cows mooing and a quad bike coming quite near, oh shit, the farmers going to tell me off for camping on his land, either that or the cows will trample me and Buddy to death in our tent. The quad bike drove off into the distance, he'd not seen us and when I opened the tent door there were cows around but they took no notice of the little green tent that had appeared overnight. I made a brew and some porridge, fed Buddy some more dried food, washed up and then packed everything away back into my back pack, a routine that was to become very familiar. So I had survived my first official wild camp, the first wild camp I had ever done with Buddy, I felt quite proud of myself as we set off again for Lynton.

With mine and Buddy's back packs slightly lighter but not much, we walked along in lovely weather, we were both enjoying our little selves. Because we hadn't reached our planned destination yesterday, I thought the best plan was to have no plan at all and just walk and see where we ended up at about 5pm to save on frustration. Even that plan failed, I was determined not to rush the walk, I couldn't walk fast anyway with a heavy bag and sore shins. I wanted to take my time and enjoy the experience, having two sticks allowed me to look at the views more without tripping up and breaking something. Buddy just did his own thing and needed no supervision, he didn't need to be on a lead, only when we got really close to a cliff edge did I have to put him on it for my own peace of mind more than anything.

By the time we got to Lynton it was 2pm! Bloody hell this walking was taking too long, instead of taking one day to reach our first destination it had taken nearly two! I was also amazed to find I was starving again and knackered already. There was only one thing to do, go to the nearest cafe and order a big fat pasty, which is what I did only to be shocked when they charged £4.90 for a pasty and an orange drink. Wow, this ain't going to be cheap but it did taste delicious and was one of many to pass my lips on the way to my hips.

I was sat on a bench opposite the Rock House Hotel reading my map book trying to decide whether I should walk to the camp site up the main road or carry on up the path. I'd been to the tourist information centre to ask if they knew if the site allowed dogs because some of them don't. They said they didn't know for sure but probably they did, very bloody helpful, I didn't want to walk up a main A road to find they didn't, so I was going to ask about buses then changed my mind knowing how Buddy didn't like them. Decisions, decisions, they are hard to make when you're knackered. It was 3pm by now and it looked like I would have to carry on and wild camp again. I was looking enviously at the smart hotel and wished I had loads of money so I could stay there in comfort and have a nice soft bed and hot shower, when the gardener from the hotel, who was swilling some dog shit off the pavement in front of me came over and started chatting. I asked him was there any other camp sites around that didn't involve a bus ride or walking on main roads, he was very helpful and for the first time I discovered that local knowledge came in very handy. He told me about a place near the town hall in Lynton, I won't tell you where it is because everyone will be descending on this spot for free camping. It took me another hour to walk there, it was up the hill past the Lynmouth Cliff railway, cliff being the clue to how steep the path was at this point. I noticed a shop in the town on the way there and after finding the spot he had told me about and pitching my tent, I walked back to the shop with an empty rucksack and filled it with loads of nice healthy food, a bag of salad and sliced ham with coleslaw, a pint of milk, cereal bars for breakfast, a two litre bottle of water as there were no streams about, a packet of peanuts and most importantly, two pint cans of my favourite lager that begins with an S and is a woman's name. It seemed like a queens' banquet.

So my second wild camp was a little more rural, no one saw us and I still felt safe with Buddy. The salad and beer were delicious if not hard to eat as I had no fork or plate, I just shoved it all in the salad wrapper and ate it like a horse with a nose bag. After the two pints, I slept like a baby for 10 hours and woke up in bright strong sunshine that soon dried my tent. I set off again heading towards Combe Martin, another long 14 mile stretch which I knew by now I'd never make. I noticed a camp site on my map about half way there, I was now desperate for a wash, I'd used the public toilets near the town hall in Lynton for my mornings ablutions (I hate that word), but really needed a proper shower.

The walk out of Lynton was fantastic, along the North Walk, Hollerday Hill and onto the Valley of the Rocks where mountain goats were grazing. I went wrong round here and ended up wasting time and energy walking up a steep hill I didn't need to walk up. I must concentrate more on my map reading. It shouldn't be difficult finding your way along the South West Coast Path, they say all you have to do is keep your right foot wet, the sea on your right and you can't go wrong. It is well sign posted most of the time, but you can go wrong if you don't pay attention. Everyone who saw Buddy smiled and then commented what a great idea it was to have the dog carry his own stuff, some asked what was in there, some asked where could they get their own dog a set, but Buddy and his packs never failed to make people smile as they passsed him. I was finding that when they saw us approaching, they first smiled at Buddy and his bags and then said something like "Isn't it a nice day" I would reply in my thickest of northern accents "Yeh init" But I was finding after the hundredth time this was asked I was becoming a little embarrassed at my reply so I found myself saying "Yes it is isn't it", this walking was turning me posh, if I keep this up I'll end up talking like the Queen "My Dog and I" wave wave!

I had set my sights lower today and was heading for a real camp site and hopefully a hot shower, but it still seemed ages and it was nearly 4pm when I reached Holdstone Farm camp site hoping that they allowed dogs and were open for business. I needn't have worried it was open and they did take dogs. The first thing I did was drink litres of water from their tap, me and Buddy together were very thirsty, it had been about 24 degrees all day and I hadn't carried enough water and had been too lazy to filter some.

I booked in with the farmer's wife, it was only £5, it was a very basic site but had hot showers that didn't need coins so I was in there for ages loving it, after 2 nights and three days of hard slog and wild camping, a shower was the best thing in the world. I washed my red Rohan shirt and my drawers and hung them out to dry in the evening sunshine, the first of many times I would do this, and they dried very quickly. I'd asked the farmers wife if she had any milk for my tea, she filled my water bottle up from her own personal 4 pint bottle of milk in her fridge and refused to be paid, such a kind gesture that for some reason really touched me and nearly had me in tears, it made me feel very humble, the first act of kindness that I came across many times as I went along the path. Later as I was cooking my noodles, the lady in the caravan next to me came over and offered me a glass of Baileys, she said she'd noticed I was backpacking on my own, something she had always wanted to do but couldn't now she had kids and a husband. She knew all about the South West Coast Path and how long it was, then she asked was I intending to walk it all and I found myself for the first time, telling a lie and I said yes I was, she was very impressed. I refused the Baileys and quite wrongly said, sorry but I can't just drink one glass, I'd have to have the whole bottle, bet she thought "the cheeky git! "

But I was using this walk as an opportunity to cut down on my alcohol consumption, a sort of detox, as a woman of my build, 5 foot nothing, I drink too much, if the weekly sum of units for a woman is supposed to be 25, I could easily consume that amount in one evening. You could say I am a heavy drinker bordering on alcoholism. Doing this long walk was a good time to keep me off it for a bit so I said no to the Baileys even though I love the stuff.

Washed and fed, Buddy and I set off the next day towards Combe Martin. When we arrived I went to the chemists for my first of many packet of Compeed, a type of blister plaster that looks like thick skin, it's the best thing since sliced bread (no I am not sponsored by Compeed). I was developing a sore spot on my left foot and past experience told me to sort it out before it turned into a blister. The next thing I did was to fill my belly with food, on this occasion, a giant sausage roll and lucozade, not very healthy I know. Buddy had developed a liking for pasties and could smell one a mile off, he would disappear and I would find him with his nose about an inch away from some ones pasty, I'd have to apologise as I pulled him away by his collar.

We camped that night at a site I had been to a year earlier, I had seen a guy there doing a long stretch of the path and remembered how jealous I was of him. This time it was me doing it, my dream had come true.

The weather was still lovely, after showering and doing my laundry, I walked back up the path to the camp site next door and had dinner in their cafe. I had a delicious pizza, then Buddy and I went into the bar, I had a pint while watching Manchester United on the big screen. I was sat on a red velvet seat, after only four days of camping and having to sit on the camp floor all the time, I was amazed at how much I missed a soft seat; I was concious of the feel of my weight on my buttocks instead of it being on the bottom of my feet . Buddy was fast asleep on the carpeted floor beside me, he was probably missing his home comforts too. We were both in heaven.

You can't get a weather forecast when you have no access to TV or internet, you have to ask people as you go along. I'd forgot to ask anyone today, I had started taking the good weather for granted a bit, I'd just finished my second pint when it started raining, I rushed out of the bar and back to my tent but managed to get wet through as I had no coat on, I never left my tent after that without my waterproofs. Getting into a tent wet is bad enough, getting into one with a wet dog as well is the pits, everything gets soaked especially after the inevitable shake, it's a good job I love my dog!

He was running out of his food so today's mission was to find him some, it had never occurred to me when I was replenishing (another word I hate) my noodles and stuff to get Buddy any, how selfish was that? What a bad owner I am! At least his bags were lighter, he was still carrying them without complaining, so when we reached Ilfracombe I took them off him and like some cartoon character taking off his clothes, he went for a swim to cool off in Ilfracombe Harbour. A lady walking her dogs came over as I sat on the sand watching him enjoying his swim, she asked all sorts of questions about my walk, was I walking all the 630 miles to Poole? I don't know why I was doing this, but I lied again and said yes I was. I had no intention of walking to Poole! Why was I lying!?

When we got to Ilfracombe town it was dinner time again, I went into a shop, I won't say which one, and replenished my emergency food. This time, I bought Buddy two of those sachets of dog food that come in tin foil and have a picture of a small dog on them. I thought they wouldn't be too heavy for him to carry, one in each side in his panniers. I also ordered for myself a jacket potato with tuna and mayo, I had to order it at the back of the shop where the ovens were and pay for it along with my other shopping at the till at the front. I had to wait 10 minutes for it to be ready; so I went outside and packed my shopping away and put Buddy's food in his bags. Buddy has always only had dried food in his 7 long years, it's better for his teeth apparently, he has never had the joy of wet dog food before so he was in for a treat.

Ten minutes later I went back in to get my spud. On the way to the back of the shop I decided to get Buddy another of these foil tins so he could eat it now as I could tell he wasn't getting enough to eat and was famished. I collected my spud and went towards the till to pay for the dog food but there was a long queue, I thought, sod it, I'm not waiting in that, my spud will go cold; well that was my excuse as I walked out of the shop without paying for it! So now I was a shoplifter as well as a liar!

CHAPTER 5
The Shoplifting Dog

It wasn't the first time I had ever shoplifted, the first time also involved a dog. His name was Patch. I was twelve years old and had already started smoking, I was dragged up, I mean brought up on a council overspill estate called Langley. My family was far from rich and pocket money was hard to come by, thrupence is what we got, you could buy a lot of sweets with that but it wasn't enough for cigarettes. You were the odd one out in school if you didn't swear and smoke so I did both to keep in with my rough, scruffy, runny nosed, unwashed peers. (That's a bit of an exaggeration but it's not far off). So to fuel my fag habit, when Mum asked for volunteers to go to the shop for our daily supply of five pounds of spuds (there were six of us to feed) and a tin of dog meat, I always offered my services. I'd walk to the shops about a mile away from our council house with my dog Patch by my side. I'd had him from being a puppy, he was my faithful dog, he didn't need a lead, he was a very independent, intelligent dog. We would both enter the shop together because in those days dogs were allowed in and there were no CCTV surveillance. At the top of the shop door was a bell on a spring that let the shopkeeper know when someone had come in or out. I would go down the isle and pick up the potatoes and a tin of dog meat. I then put the tin in the dogs mouth just like a bone and Patch would walk to the door and wait patiently until someone came in or went out, he would then go out the door and go straight home with this tin of meat in his mouth. It was a bit cruel because he had to cross a main road and I wouldn't do it now. I, in the meantime, had heard the bell go and knew Patch had gone out and I just walked to the counter and paid for the spuds only. What a scam, I was only 12 years old and four foot nothing. Whether the owner knew what was going on I will never know, but the dog meat cost ten and a half pence which was exactly the price of ten park drive and a book of matches from the off licence opposite, I would walk home, five pound of spuds in one hand and a fag in the other, puffing away, smoking my head off. Patch never failed to get his tin home and leave it on our front lawn, I didn't teach him to do all this, he just did it himself. So this went on for a while and was my first experience of stealing things, but of course it wasn't me doing the shoplifting, it was my dog, honest mister!

Another way to raise money for my fag fund was another scam involving doing my Mums washing. She would send me to the laundrette with two big black bags full of dirty laundry. One full of whites, and one full of colours which I put in a pram and pushed uphill to the laundrette. I was still only twelve, talk about child labour, but it wasn't like that because I volunteered for this job too. We couldn't afford a washing machine at the time so Mum gave me enough money for two washes, two spins and two loads of driers. I would not only shove the whites and colours in one machine to save money for my fags, but it all went in one drier as well, Mum sometimes questioned why some of the whites were a ghoulish grey colour and why was all the washing still a bit damp, I just shrugged my shoulders and went for a fag. She never knew I smoked, or she didn't let on if she did and I was gutted when one day I came home from school and found out my Dad had bought my Mum a new shiny white washing machine and he'd had to have Patch put down because he'd bitten a kid!

I had only walked 40 miles of the South West Coast Path and it had taken me five and a half days! Some people could do that in two! I was going too slow and it was embarrassing, if I got to an uphill bit I'd be even slower, 20 paces and I would have to stop to get my breath back, the bag was too heavy. I'd get hot and sweaty too and had to take my base ball cap off to let out the heat from my head, the cap had been hiding my greasy wet hair and with steam coming out of my ears, I looked like the wild woman of Wonga. One woman approached me as I struggled slowly up another set of steps, I hadn't noticed her. I had took my cap off to let my head cool, she looked at me a little concerned and asked "Are you all right love, you look a bit hot". I know they say the path's ascent and descent totals three Everest's but this was ridiculous. The path would send you up a hundred steps and then when you reached the top it would send you back down again just like the Grand Old Duke of York! Every body was walking faster than me, parents, children, grandparents even a snail past me at one point. So I started lying to people who past me who asked when I had started the walk at Minehead, I would lie and say three days ago.

So with my hot potato and my stolen dog food that I had got from the shop in Ilfracombe, we headed for a shed in the posh gardens of a nearby hotel because it looked like it was going to rain. I found a sun lounger in there and lay down like lady muck and ate my delicious spud while Buddy devoured his stolen booty. I watched a seagull stomping up and down on the grass opposite while I ate, it was making the worms think it was raining, I've only ever seen blackbirds do this, I have never seen a seagull do it, it looked quite comical. Then it did rain, hard, people started running from the beach back into their posh hotel, I watched them with envy, being able to go indoors and get dry, I was beginning to feel like a homeless tramp.

It stopped raining and the sun came out so we carried on up the path towards Woolacombe, it was 1pm and I could tell from my map there were no camp sites further up the path or here in Ilfracombe, we could stay here in a B & B but it was too early and I was too tight to pay for one anyway, so I decided to carry on and see what happened, our bags were full of emergency food so we could just keep going. I think that's what you call freedom, to be self sufficient, it was a great feeling, helped of course by the sunny weather. We came across some National Trust land near Bull Point about 4 miles on, it overlooked the sea and was ideal for a wild camp. It was quiet, had a stream and some flat grass with no cows, just sheep, the view out to sea was fantastic, I watched the ships slowly go by as I cooked my noodles and custard, Buddy thought it was Christmas when he got more of the

41

wet dog food. I slept again like a baby and maybe because it was so quiet or maybe because I was knackered, I woke again 12hrs later. I was doing more sleeping than walking, and it was taking an age to pack up and get going, no wonder it was taking so long, but there was no rush, I was after all, here to enjoy the ride not just do it for the sake of it. I have to broach the subject of what a wild camper has to do when there is no toilet available, those of you with weak stomachs and all you ladies of a disposition please skip to the next chapter.

First of all, you have to carry spare toilet roll which is no problem as it doesn't weigh much, the trouble is keeping it dry. Then if you find yourself in the middle of nowhere needing the loo and I don't mean for a wee, you have no choice but to go behind a bush and have a squat like someone sat on an invisible toilet, this requires strong thigh muscles. I am an expert wild wee-er, I have wee'd thousands of times in the outdoors, baring my arse to the world is no problem I drop my drawers at every pause! But doing the other is something a lady should never have to do or at least confess to but it's a fact of life when you are wild camping, when you've gotta go, you've gotta go. Enough said.

Today's destination was Croyde where I knew there were two camp sites to choose from. We walked past Woolacombe sands that seemed to go on for ages, over Baggy Point and into Croyde. This is where I made my first mistake. The owner of the camp site told me they didn't allow dogs and he owned the other site here too and that one didn't take dogs either. It would be too expensive to go into a B & B here he told me, he also said the nearest camp site that allowed dogs was 4 miles inland up a main A road. What a cock up, I didn't know what to do, I was again knackered and so was Buddy, but the owner kindly came to the rescue and gave us a lift to the dog friendly camp site. He took us in his open backed land rover, me in the passenger seat with Buddy on my knee. As he drove off a bit erratically (he was a busy man and was in a rush), Buddy decided he didn't like being on my knee near the windscreen and started going berserk trying to jump out of the window. By the time we arrived at the site at Braunton, my legs were full of bruises caused by Buddy's stressful clawing and my favourite Buffalo wind shirt was ripped.

The kind owner drove off and I booked in, the wardens recognised my thick northern accent and asked where was I from? I told them Rochdale, they were from the next town of Heywood, what a small world, from then on we were looked after, what a nice couple they were. They asked all about my walk and couldn't believe I was doing it on my own, albeit with a dog, they asked the inevitable question, was I going to the end at Poole? It was becoming ridiculous because I lied again, was I trying to impress my northern neighbours?

I put my tent up and got cleaned up, then walked into the town and filled my rucksack up with two days worth of food and beer for me and tins of dog food for Buddy. Tomorrow I planned to walk inland back to Croyde and then walk back to my tent on the bit of the path I had missed out. I didn't want to miss even one step of the path out, I don't know why, maybe it was a bit anal (another hated word). This meant staying here two nights and doing extra miles but it had to be done, another day wasted, what a cock up!

The next bit of the path from Braunton was not very pleasant, the South West Coast Path goes way way inland via the Tarka Trail on an old disused railway line that's been turned into a cycle path. It goes on and on, not for miles but for days, well that's how long it took me. Cycling on a cycle path is very pleasant, walking on it with a heavy pack is not. I did not enjoy it at all. I broke up the monotony of it by stopping off at a cafe, one of those greasy spoon ones next to an industrial estate. I wasn't expecting much but I was again bloody starving. I ordered a full English breakfast, borrowed their newspaper and sat outside in the sun reading the Sun. It was the best fry up I have ever had.

The kind wardens at Braunton had looked on the internet and had found a B & B a days walk away that had a spare single room and allowed dogs (it was still peak season) but it would cost £42! I didn't book it but just carried on walking to see what happened. At the end of the day at 5pm after endless miles of flat boring walking, we were approaching this B & B when it started raining. There was obviously nowhere to wild camp here so I decided to bite the bullet and pay through the nose for a soft bed, it would be Buddy's first ever B & B. I knocked on the door, the owner wasn't too pleased to see a wet dog and an even wetter walker standing there dripping, wanting a room. I asked him for a towel which he reluctantly gave me and I wiped Buddy down as best I could with it, I even gave my hat a rub for a laugh, but he didn't see the funny side, he showed us to this tiny room just as Buddy decided to shake mud and water all over him and his new carpets.

I fed Buddy with his emergency supplies then he fell asleep on the carpeted floor and didn't move for 12hrs, he was knackered. There were no shops for miles and nowhere to eat out unless you had a car so I cooked my noodles in this very posh 4 star room which didn't seem quite right really considering I had to keep wafting the steam away so I didn't set off the fire alarm. The milk was downstairs in a communal fridge, on one side there was a sign which read – You are never too old to know better – and another on the other side read – My husband is the boss around here and he has my permission to say it.

Back in the room the bed was luxuriously soft and warm, the TV was a real treat from which I got a weather forecast, it was OK for a few days then they predicted very heavy rain. Next day and more of the bloody cycle path, over the bridge at Bideford where I filled up Buddy's packs with about 2kgs of dried food, he was getting more and more comments on how cute he looked, some people even took pictures of him.

It was here we met a couple who asked me the same question - was I walking the whole 630 miles to Poole? I was getting used to lying now and just automatically said yes. I had no intention of doing it all, Padstow was my destination or Land's End if possible, at this pace it would take me forever to reach Poole. They were so impressed they asked where was I staying that evening, I said I wasn't sure, just anywhere where we could camp. They kindly gave me their name, address and telephone number and said if I wanted, me and Buddy could stay at their house in Westward Ho! How lovely and kind, this never happens to me normally, just because we were doing this walk, people were being so kind in all sorts of ways. I told them I would only take up their offer in an emergency, thanked them and walked on up the cycle way into Appledoor and by 5pm we had reached Westward Ho! where they lived, it's the only town with a ! in its name. There is a golf course there with a visitor's centre that had a tap outside and toilets that opened up at 9am. I won't go into detail but I never took up the couple's kind offer – I found somewhere else to stay if you get my drift.

It was tough going next day as we headed for Clovelly, I don't know why but I found it really hard work, up and down the path went, then up some more, it was my toughest day so far. I don't know if it was the humidity or what but I really struggled, I sweated and puffed my way along and the bag felt even heavier than usual. I was going unbelievably slow, it felt like I was taking one step forward and two steps back. I had worked out I had been doing a pathetic one mile an hour so far along the walk, today I was going even slower, it's a good job I was on my own and had no one to complain about my pace. Anyone swimming along side me in the sea would have gone faster, the path kept going up and then down to sea level, at least Buddy got a cooling swim out of it, I would have joined him but I didn't have a proper towel, just a square piece of light weight pertex that I used when I showered, Tony has got one as well and he says they are as much use as a chocolate fire guard.

I only managed 8 miles before I came to a complete stop nowhere near Clovelly but near a holiday village just past Buck's Mills. I was too tired, I couldn't go on any further so I found a flat piece of ground next to a picnic table and hid my bag that I was so sick of carrying by now, all I wanted to do was give it a kick. I walked into the holiday village, with the weight of the bag now off my shoulders I felt very light, like a helium balloon, it was a weird sensation. There were no camping facilities at the village just a load of chalets, but a nice man filled two of his empty wine bottles with tap water for me so I didn't have to use my filter as there were no streams about. I carried these bottles back to my bag looking like some alcoholic tramp, wishing they were actually full of wine not water, but beggars can't be choosers. I put my tent up next to the table and made dinner which I enjoyed sat on a seat for a change and not on the camp floor.

I had met a very overweight (fat) bloke with a huge towering rucksack on his back today going even slower than me. He too, he told me, was backpacking on the South West Coast Path but for only two weeks, I noticed his roll up mat still had the cellophane on it. When I told him I had done about 100 miles from Minehead he was very impressed and said he would be very pleased if he could do that much in the two weeks he had. He said he had lost his water bottle so I gave him some of my water as it was a very hot day and he was sweating more than me and I could use my water filter to get more. He told me he was suffering from a bad back , I left him and carried on, thinking he would pass by my camping spot later on. I didn't see him pass, I came across him next day ahead of me walking out of Clovelly. I wondered how he had managed to get ahead of me knowing how slow he walked, then I noticed the cellophane was still on his mat, he obviously hadn't camped but when I asked him he admitted he had caught a bus yesterday back to his B & B because he was so knackered and had caught a bus back to Clovelly that morning. I thought what a cheat and what a nutter, this is probably the worst thing he could be doing with a bad back, walking on this difficult terrain carrying that huge heavy rucksack, but obviously I didn't voice my opinions to his face; who was I to tell him what to do, it would have been like the kettle calling the pot black. I never saw him again after that, I wonder how he went on?

I would have loved to have gone down into Clovelly as it is supposed to be a nice place to visit and if you aren't in a car its free but I was too tired to walk down from the path only to have to walk back up again. I promised myself I would come back one day and take a look.

After two consecutive wild camps I was again desperate for a shower. Anyone who can't do without their daily shower should look away now or skip to the next page. After three days of sweating I headed for the next camp site on my map the only problem was it was 11 miles away but I had no choice, I couldn't bear the thought of another shower less night. Luckily the going was slightly easier and the last two miles were down hill into Hartland Quay. People were still smiling at Buddy's back packs and commenting on what a good idea they were, it was all wearing a bit thin now as I was getting more and more tired, the novelty of their compliments was wearing off. I had to make sure I stood down wind of anybody who stopped to talk to me, I was very concious of how much I stank. It was a long 14 mile day but I made it to the camp site and had an endless shower, I even 'borrowed' a real towel that someone had washed and had left drying in the barn where the showers were (sorry about that if it was your towel). Buddy who was now tucked up in bed was running out of food again so I asked the owner did they have a shop or any for sale to which they replied no to both but she did give me some milk for nowt and told me there was a shop in the village.

The next day was gloriously sunny and warm and after yesterdays gruelling 14 miler I was in need of a rest. So because I was in no rush and was a lazy git, I had my first rest day, after all, as Louis Armstrong sings, I had all the time in the woilrld. I sat about doing nothing, the joy of not moving was wonderful. I just lay in the sun with Buddy for hours then did some laundry and decided to walk to the village shop for some food supplies.

We set off with an empty rucksack and walked into Hartland Quay about a mile away thinking that was the village where the owner had said there was a shop.

There was a shop there but it was just a bloody souvenir shop, the village she had meant was Harland not Harland Quay which was about 3 miles inland up the main road. Bugger! It is frustrating when you haven't got a car, you may as well be in the desert, you feel so isolated even with people milling around. The car I take for granted at home would have come in handy right now and I would just nip up the road to the shop just like that and not even think about it. I walked back to my tent with an empty bag and stomach feeling dejected. Another Good Samaritan, the guy in the next tent who was a male nurse from welsh Wales, I can't remember his name, came to my rescue when I told him my predicament. He kindly gave me a lift to the shop while his wife minded Buddy. When he found out I was walking the South West Coast Path, he told me he was jealous and had always wanted to do it and may still do in the future with his son if he ever got the chance. I quickly filled my rucksack with lovely food both human and dog. I got some beer for me and gas for my camping stove, I was conscious of him waiting outside with his engine running and didn't want to make him wait or he might drive off and leave me here in the middle of nowhere. It was very kind of him and I'd like to now thank him, there can't be that many male nurses in Wales who give lifts to strange woman so you know who you are.

I had also got a newspaper and read it in the evening sunshine back at the tent, the five day forecast wasn't good, heavy rain was coming overnight. And it did! Talk about heavy rain, I had been lucky up to now with the weather, there is something quite mystical about being in a tent when it's raining and you are tucked up in bed, nice and warm and dry but it's not the same with heavy rain, it sounded so loud it woke me up, at least it didn't thunder, Buddy hates that.

I should never have set off next day, but the stubborn git that I am made me get up and go, there was no way I wanted another day off, that would be really lazy. It was pouring with rain as I packed up my tent, luckily I could take the inner tent down and pack my bag while still inside the outer tent. Past experience has taught me to always make sure you keep your sleeping bag and inner tent as dry as possible (keep your tinder dry). So Buddy and I kept dry till the last minute then reluctantly we had to go out into the rain and pack up my now heavy with rain, outer tent. My rucksack had a waterproof cover so hopefully that would keep some of the rain out. I was wearing my trusted Paramo waterproofs and had on some goretex boots and some new untested seal skin gloves so for the first few hours I stayed dry.

The rain got heavier and heavier, it was that bad at one point I couldn't see through it, it was coming down in sheets. We came to a stream that is normally crossed by some round stepping stones above a waterfall that runs into the sea. The stepping stones were under water as the stream had now turned into a raging river, I had to take my shoes and socks off and roll my trousers up so I could wade across, I took my bag off, put Buddy on his lead and took him across first, the water was up to my knees and quite strong, I used one of my sticks for balance. Buddy nearly got washed away because it was up to his shoulders and it was threatening to take him over the waterfall and into the sea never to be seen again! With him over safely I had to go back and get my bag and do it all again, it was more difficult with the weight and Buddy was trying to get back to me, I had to scream at him to stop so he could hear me over the noise of the water and rain, it was all a bit hairy. I made it over and put my shoes and socks back on. To get out of the rain, we had lunch in Ronald Duncan's hut, there were free copies of his books in containers on the floor. I would have loved to have taken one to read but my bag was heavy enough and was getting heavier because everything was getting wet through. We then carried on, I was pleased because we had now entered my beloved Cornwall, the rain never relented and it was getting windy as well. It got to 4pm and we were both soaked to the skin, my supposedly waterproof boots had water running through them, even my knickers were wet. I'd had enough, we were nowhere near any civilisation and I was piss wet through so I decided to put my tent up near a stream. I put the outer tent up first to get out of the rain and we both got in, Buddy had a few good shakes. I was sat on my bag dripping and Buddy was stood up looking at me like Stan Laurel saying – another fine mess you've gotten me into! -. Then he did something I have never seen him do – he started shivering and chattering his teeth – shit I thought, this is serious, we are both going to die of hypothermia. This was a real Ray Mears survival situation! We had drip dried a little bit so I put up the inner tent, Buddy got on his bed and I covered him with my Paramo coat and then I got into my sleeping bag which thank the lord was the only dry thing I owned. It was only 4.30 pm. It was too wild and wet to cook, even to make a cup of tea but we both soon warmed up and later had something to eat. This was the first time I was a bit scared, it was going dark, still raining and blowing a gale, I felt very alone, I put on my ipod and watched the film Camelot with the earphones in so I couldn't hear the horrible weather outside, this made me feel a little better.

I awoke next day and it had stopped raining thank God. I still had to put my wet shoes and socks on, it was like wearing cold wet porridge. We walked towards Bude and had a late breakfast in the first cafe we came across, sat there in wet footwear the food tasted divine. I was looking forward to getting to our next camp site to dry off. We camped at a site on the other side of Bude, I had been there last year and saw a woman on her own, obviously backpacking the South West Coast Path, looking knackered, this time it was me looking knackered, but I was loving it despite our few near misses yesterday.

CHAPTER 6
My Date With A Grid

I rang Kevin to see if he was coming down to join us, he told me parts of south Wales and southern Cornwall had been flooded, I could well understand why, I had experienced the worst rain I have ever had the displeasure to walk in and had survived but it was a close call. He said he would meet us at Tintagel further on up the path. I had stuffed my shoes with newspaper overnight and washed and dried everything in the dryer. So I set off with dry feet and underwear, luxury, towards Cracklington Haven. I was walking along minding my own business when a woman with her long haired Labrador approached us, I looked up just as her dog made a B line to attack Buddy, we were near a cliff edge and for a split second I thought Buddy was a goner. Just as all this happened, even with two sticks either side of me, I managed to find a rabbit hole with my left foot and fell down it, the weight of my bag dragged me down and I ended up on my back like a stranded tortoise. It was a good job anyway because all this commotion distracted the Labrador and stopped him attacking Buddy. I lay there and thought I had twisted my left ankle, shit. End of walk! The woman came over and looked down at me, I looked up at her, she asked was I OK to which I would like to have replied - No I am not! Your stupid dog has done this and now I won't be able to walk – but of course I didn't say that, I just said - I am OK I just need to lie here for a bit while my ankle recovers – she just said OK and walked off with her dog, leaving me on the floor with a possible broken ankle, thanks a lot love!

It was not the worst fall I have ever had, the worst and most embarrassing one was when I was about 17 years old. I had a date with a guy called Dave. He had carrot red hair and suffered terribly with bad acne. I was very good looking in those days even though I say it myself, so why I went out with him I don't know, maybe it was because he had a car. I dolled myself up in my sisters clothes, make up and perfume. I borrowed her fur coat and her long maxi skirt that went down to my ankles and hid my spindly white legs. I was looking beautiful and smelt lovely. He knocked on the door and we walked down our path, me in my sister's brown fur coat and him looking like a match stick, we turned right to walk about 10 yards to where his black shiny Capri was parked. He got in the Capri and lent over and unlocked the passenger door for me, I had to bend down to open the door as it's a very low car. I was just about to step in when it happened - Unknowingly to me, someone had kindly nicked the grid lid from the roadside drain and I fell down it! It happened so quickly, I found myself in this muddy, dirty, slimy, oily drain. I would have gone straight down but I had managed to stop myself with my elbows. As you know when you fall over, you try to get up as quickly as possible and pretend it hasn't happened. I would have liked to have got out and pretend it hadn't happened but I couldn't climb out, my legs couldn't get any purchase on the slimy sides of the drain. The drain hole was about an inch short of my hip width so as I went down I managed to scrape a layer of skin off my hips and thighs. So there I was, up to my elbows, my skirt round my neck with my legs dangling in mud and slime and I couldn't get out.

He had just got in his car and had unlocked the passenger door, when he looked again I had disappeared, he thought - where's she gone? - Then he looked down and saw my head on level with the passenger seat! He rushed round the back of the car and by the scruff of the neck of my fur coat he dragged me out like a wet dog and put me back on the pavement. I pulled my skirt down from around my neck and tried to hide my embarrassment by asking him to wait there while I went back home to tidy myself up, I limped indignantly back to my house. In the bathroom I found I had scraped my knees, thighs and hips and they were caked in blood and mud, my tights were full of holes and ladders. Surprisingly all I did was wash my hands and went back out with him

We went out for a meal which was spoilt when his acne started popping when he was eating and it was knocking me sick. Apart from that we had a lovely evening until I tried to get up, I had seized up, all the scrapes and bruises were killing me, I must have looked like a 90 year old as I tried to walk back to his car. He took me home and I never saw him again. Next day I was lay on the couch licking my wounds, I couldn't walk and had huge bruises on my thighs. Our neighbour Mrs Mills came in and saw me lying there, she asked me how I was, I said – OK thanks – then she asked me was I sure, to which I replied - Yes I am OK thanks – she then asked me how my date went, I replied – Fine thanks – then she started laughing and said she had seen it all happen. Typical nosey neighbour, from behind the curtains, she had seen me walk out with this guy and had seen me fall down the grid! She said she hadn't stopped laughing since!

Back on the South West Coast Path, I lay there on my rucksack and massaged my ankle, the woman and her dog nonchalantly walked away, I think she was feeling guilty and wanted to get away before I sued her. I got up and my ankle felt fine, a miracle! I could continue my walking. We wild camped just before Cracklington Haven overlooking the sea again near a waterfall, this was great, all this free camping, this trip wasn't turning out as expensive as I thought, I had hardly touched my £2500 bank account. It reminded me of that song by Seasick Steve where he sings – I started out with nothing and I still have most of it left.

I had only just noticed how thin Buddy had become, I had been stuffing myself with extra food loaded with calories while I was just giving him his normal amount, he was doing extra exercise as well and was burning up energy too, so when I ordered a pasty and salad next day at the cafe in Cracklington Haven I asked did they have anything a dog could eat, they only had premium sausages, so I ordered two of them for him. The cook was shocked to see me give her best sausage to a dog. Food tastes one hundred times better after miles of hard slog and wild camps and you just can't get enough of it, I knew I was losing weight too but I was pleased with that, maybe I might loose some of that middle age spread I've been trying to get rid of for years. I sat there reading the cafe's newspaper eating the best pasty in the world. It was great being able to eat all this food and calories and not put weight on, it was like being a bulimic without having to throw up afterwards.

Kevin was due to meet us in two days so I took it easy and didn't do many miles, I chatted to a local man who said he was a seal monitor, he lent me his binoculars to look at a seal colony. I would have just walked past them because they were camouflaged against the rocks out at sea, he told me some seals are a ginger colour when young. He also told me there was a farm camp site just inland near Boscastle. When I got there, the site wasn't much to write home about, the showers were freezing and they had no shop or milk, so it was noodles and custard again for tea. I was getting bloody sick of them now, there are more minerals and vitamins in the wrapper than in the noodles, I was going to end up with rickets, I made a mental note to get some fruit and veg down me and feed Buddy up before Kevin came down and saw how skeletal he'd become.

At Boscastle, the now famous village that got flash flooded in 2004, I stopped at a cafe and had a big fat fry up, this trip was turning out to be a constant battle of getting food and finding a shower! I bought Buddy a large tin of wet dog food and opened it into a carrier bag as I had no bowl. His eyes were out on stalks as he ate it like a horse with a nose bag. There is a pretty little Youth Hostel here that would have been nice to stay in but they don't allow dogs.

With full belly's we set off for Tintagel, along the way I met a couple of women walking towards us, one of them, they told me, had walked all the way from Poole and was heading for Minehead to complete the whole 630 mile South West Coast Path! This was the first person I had met who was walking the whole path, I was green with envy, and she was a woman as well, she only looked about 19 years old, I thought what a brave young girl. She said she had also been doing loads of wild camping and it was her 31st day and she hoped to finish in about another 10 days. So I wasn't the only daft woman doing this sort of thing. She was walking with her mother who was keeping her company for a bit. I wished her luck, she needed it because I knew what was coming up for her, all that up and down, all those steep climbs and steps she had to endure. It had taken me 17 days to get here but of course I lied. When they asked when had I started at Minehead? I said "12 days ago" I also lied and said I too was walking the whole path. She was quite impressed with that and the fact I was doing it with a dog as well. I wondered had she lied too about how long it had taken her but no, it's only me who is dishonest, I am sure she was telling the truth.

Tintagel is a lovely spot with lots of history, if you ever get the chance, you should visit. When I arrived, after booking in at the town's camp site where I had arranged to meet Kevin, I walked into town, there were plenty of shops, takeaways and more pubs than you can shake a stick at. I filled my bag up with all my favourites and had a feast that night in my tent.

Kevin arrived at 10am next day, he had driven overnight to beat the traffic, we spent the day exploring Tintagel and it's castle. He had never been to Cornwall before. Luckily the weather was fantastic and was forecast to stay like that all week while he was there. He put his tent up then we went shopping in the town for barbecue stuff and beers, time for me and Buddy to feed ourselves up. Kevin was shocked at how much weight Buddy had lost, he looked like a bag of bones, I felt like I had been neglecting him, I obviously hadn't been feeding him enough, so over the next five days Buddy got extra portions and more and so did I.

My car was still in Porlock, so next day Kevin drove us back and I paid £36 to the camp site owner because at £2 per day, I had been walking for 18 days. We took both cars to my usual haunt of Crantock. When I told the owner of the camp site there that I was walking on the South West Coast Path, he let me park my car in his camping field for nothing. After all, I was a regular customer and had been going there for six years now. So I planned to continue walking from Tintagel to Crantock and maybe finish walking there and just do my usual thing or carry on until Land's End or even better, finish at Falmouth which is where my second map book finished. It all depended on how Buddy and I felt and of course the weather.

We went to the lovely village pub in Crantock, there are two but I have my favourite, we had a meal and Kevin had a few beers as I had agreed to drive his car back to Tintagel, I was just enjoying feeding my face, having a soft seat and driving instead of walking.

I had another day off next day to show Kev some of Cornwall's sights. We visited his first ever Cornish beach at Trebarwith Strand. We just sat there and watched the giant waves crashing in. Then we drove to Boscastle for lunch as I had noticed they had a gluten free menu, Kev is gluten intolerant, that's probably why he is as thin as a rake, he has to eat healthy stuff because he has no choice. We stuffed ourselves again then went for a walk inland just for the sake of it, it was like I was having a bus man's holiday. Later we went back to our tents for an evening barbecue.

Kevin said he wouldn't mind having Buddy while I did more of the South West Coast Path, so next day, with a light day sack full of waterproofs, fresh sandwiches and a nice drink instead of stale bread, cheese and filtered river water. I set off on my own, which was great, I only had myself to think of, I was happy as Larry whoever he is. We had said we would base ourselves in Tintagel for 5 days and I could walk light weight until I reached the end of my first map book at Padstow. Kevin was to pick me up at the end of the day at Port Gaverne, 9 miles away. Today's walk had 7 steep valleys to cross, I was glad I didn't have my heavy sack on, crushing down on my skeleton, I found it easy going. A local man asked was I going all the way to Poole, I lied, and said yes again, it was getting beyond a joke now, he asked was I keeping a diary and I said "No, it's all getting stored in my head".

At the end of the day I arrived at the place where Kev said he'd pick me up, I was early, so I went into a pub and ordered a refreshing cool orange drink, it had been a hot day, I sat out side in the early evening sun and put my feet up and pulled my cap over my face to shield it from the strong sunshine. I was lay there enjoying not moving when a bloke came up and said "Is this chair taken sonny?"- he was talking to me? I lifted my cap off my face and said "No it's not taken and by the way I am a girl". He apologised and said "Sorry, it was the cap". I made a mental note to try and dress a little more feminine but knew I couldn't because all I had with me was my walking clothes and to be honest I didn't give a rats arse how I looked.

Kevin picked me up then dropped me off next day, I walked from Port Gaverne to Rock near Padstow or as the locals call it 'Padstein' because of Rick Stein and his hard to get into sea food restaurant. It was nearly 13 miles, the furthest I'd walked so far in one day. Again it was easy without a heavy bag. That evening we went to the pub in Tintagel and had a meal and a few pints of the black stuff, only 3 pints, my record is 8 pints in one evening, that's a lot for a woman and I am not bragging, never again! I was so ill the next day and I had dreamt I was a guini, a creature with a black body and a white head and in the morning I couldn't taste the toothpaste on my toothbrush.

Next day, it was time for Kevin to go home so he dropped me and Buddy off at Padstow. He drove off reluctantly, I think he had really enjoyed his first trip to the south and was quite impressed with what little he had seen of Cornwall, he told me he would like to come down next year for a camping holiday.

It was Buddy and I on our own again, he had his packs on full of food. I hadn't missed an inch of the path so far, as in life, if a thing is worth doing, it's worth doing properly. I didn't want to miss any of the path out, no short cuts, it's that bloody word again – anal -.

We walked through the busy streets of Padstein, around the picturesque harbour, people were once again smiling at Buddy as he walked past them with his green packs on, some were smiling and pointing at him especially children, some took pictures of him, we must have looked a strange pair, me with my large backpack and two sticks and Buddy with his panniers. But it still amazed me how he was making everyone who passed him smile.

There were a few more backpackers about, it wasn't just me, I could tell them a mile off with their huge backpacks and weary gait. I looked forward to getting away from the crowds and into the wilderness and beauty of the South West Coast Path. I had a new book in my pocket, the second of four, Padstow to Falmouth (169 miles). We were now walking towards my car at Crantock not away from it, this gave me a little security, knowing if it all went pear shaped, I could just hop in a taxi and go to Crantock.

That evening at 4pm we found ourselves at Mother Ivey Bay, which is a lovely spot with a pristine white sandy beach that overlooks the new Padstow lifeboat station. My mothers name was Ivy, so it appealed to me to stay at the camp site there, I won't say what the site was called but they know who they are, the robbing buggers (yes, I can say that, it's my book). I walked into the reception and was pleased to find they allowed dogs but was not very pleased when they wanted to charge me £21! - An extra-ordinate amount for a backpacker-. I had no choice, too tired to walk any further, they had me by the balls, I paid through the nose with my debit card, the receptionist apologised as she took my money, she said she had to do it as it was a privately owned site. I asked her did the owner wear a face mask and was he called Dick Turpin because I definitely felt like it was daylight robbery. To add insult to injury, it rained all through the night and half of the next morning.

With heavy rain next morning, I put Buddy in the laundry room to keep him dry while I packed up, then went in the site shop and bought croissants and doughnuts for breakfast, not very healthy I know. I joined Buddy in the laundry and sat watching a woman doing some ironing as I ate my stash, fancy coming on holiday and having to do ironing I thought as I stuffed a doughnut in my mouth.

We carried on towards Mawgan Porth via Bedruthan steps. This was familiar ground to me as I had walked here many times before. The going was easy, I was either getting fitter or after the steep up and downs of north Devon, the terrain was flatter, I did lots of miles this day. The weather was dry and bright, I was enjoying the walking not fighting it as I had been doing up to now. I shouldn't have been enjoying it this much considering I was roughing it in a tent with a smelly. moulting dog, Buddy had decided it was time to change his fur coat for another, my tent was full of hairs. Nevertheless, I felt I was born to do this. I have never been a girlie girl, wearing pink and frills. I have always been a tom boy, this backpacking suited me down to the ground, I was in my element. My idea of happiness is being able to do what you want, when you want and with whom you want. I was doing all three, walking the greatest long distance walk in the world (allegedly), I was doing it now and I was doing it with my faithful dog Buddy.

CHAPTER 7
A Scruffy Little Urchin Like Me

The constant task of finding food was eased at Mawgan Porth, we camped there for a more reasonable price of £5, there were plenty of takeaways and shops. I gorged myself on pizza and lager. We woke up next day to pouring rain again, it was too wet to make a brew so I got a very unhealthy breakfast from the local deli, a Danish pastry which was naughty but nice, swilled down with a pint of milk. It rained and rained all day, that heavy torrential rain that soaked me through again, the river was once again flowing through my boots, my drawers got wet and I didn't know it at the time, but my down sleeping bag was getting soaked as well, the plastic bag it was in had sprung a leak. We walked through the rain, Buddy wasn't impressed, his bags were getting soaked as well and were getting heavier and heavier, it was the first time I saw him complain. We reached Newquay, I sat and had lunch in a shelter out of the rain, it was a bit depressing sat there in wet drawers and socks but I knew we would reach my car at Crantock today so long as we could cross the river Gannel, the river that had caught me out all those years ago. There are about 4 or five ways to cross the river depending on tide times and times of year, it's all a bit complicated if you're not familiar with the area, but I was a bloody expert as I'd been coming here for years now. This time I knew all about tides, bridges and seasonal ferries. I decided to go for the ferry at Fern Pit, if the tide was out, I knew I could walk over the bridge, if it was in, I could catch the little ferry that I knew was still running.

The only problem was I knew Buddy didn't like ferries, he'd developed a dislike for them last year on the Fowey ferry, he had screamed like a baby on it, it was quite embarrassing, I had to make excuses for him and tell everyone on the boat that he had never been on one before while I held on tightly to him as he tried to jump overboard and swim for it. The Fern Pit ferry is a small one man boat, the ferry man was very understanding when I warned him Buddy might kick off when he got in the boat. My suspicions were right, Buddy once again screamed all the way over and tried to jump ship, luckily it is only a 2 minute journey, Buddy jumped out onto the familiar Crantock beach and seemed to immediately know where he was, his stress was soon forgotten.

I reached the camp site I had used so many times over the years, my car was there safe and sound, full of my base camping equipment like a brand new blow up box bed and tins of food, it was like having a stash of treasure. I set up camp and blew up the more comfortable bed by mouth as I had no foot pump, it took ages but I knew it would be worth it. To my horror I found my down sleeping bag was absolutely soaked through, if this would have happened last time I got a soaking when I was in the middle of nowhere, it would have been serious, I would have been in big trouble and I would have had to abandon my walk. Luckily I had a spare sleeping bag in the car and used that one while the lightweight down one dried out in the car.

I got cleaned up and drove to the big supermarket in town to get my favourite salad and stuff, going in the car was weird. The thought of stopping the walk now didn't cross my mind, neither did having a day off to spend it on the beach, I was enjoying the backpacking so much I wanted to carry on, so when the owner allowed me to leave my car in his field while I walked to Land's End, there was no stopping me. I told another lie here, I told him I was stopping at Land's End and would return for my car but I was secretly hoping I could reach Falmouth.

I had a very comfortable nights sleep on my cushy blow up bed. Overnight everything had dried out so I got ready to pack up and go again, I pulled the plug out of the new bed and sat on it while it deflated as I made a brew. Buddy was fast asleep behind me, the kettle had boiled. I looked behind me and saw the tent was filled with smoke, my worst nightmare had come true, I'd set fire to the tent! Shit! I jumped up knocking boiling water everywhere and dragged Buddy out quickly, he looked at me as if to say, hold on what's the rush, where's the fire. I dived back in looking for flames but there were none, it dawned on me that the 'smoke' was coming from the plug hole in the bed, it looked like white dust, when I read the bed packaging it warned of chalk dust used in the manufacture! So it wasn't smoke, just chalk dust, there was tons of it coming out, panic over.

I set off, chalk dust everywhere, I looked like a ghost and my hair had turned grey, I was walking away from my car again. I left my other two books, Falmouth to Exmouth (169 miles) and Exmouth to Poole (only! 117 miles) in the car. My new destination was Falmouth, the weather had dried up and everything was fine and dandy.

A guy walking towards me stopped and started talking, he knew all about the South West Coast Path, how long it was, how hard it was to walk it all in one go, he said he admired me for walking on my own with a dog, he asked was I doing it all and I said "maybe, I don't know" he then said "I bet there's not many women that have walked the whole path on their own with a dog", he could almost see the light bulb on the top of my head being lit. I carried on, deep in thought, what if I could reach Falmouth and carry on 'till Exmouth! And if I could reach Exmouth why not go the whole hog and go for Poole!! I got quite excited at the thought and had to stop myself daydreaming about doing the whole of the South West Coast Path in one go! More people have climbed Everest than walked the South West Coast Path without breaking off (allegedly), what a feat it would be, a dream come true, a scruffy little urchin like me from a council overspill estate doing the whole walk, if I could do it, it would even put doing Mont Blanc in the shade.

I had walked over a quarter of the South West Coast Path and was still going strong, I daydreamed all day as I walked along Perran beach which seemed to go on forever, I went through it in my mind what I would have to do to be able to finish at Poole. Then I would wake up miles later and realise I was still going at a snails pace and was just near Perranporth which was still a whooping 450 miles way from Poole, I'd tell myself off for daydreaming and told myself to not take anything for granted, to take one day at a time and baring mishaps, maybe my dream could come true. I got this deluded idea to walk the whole 630 mile path and then write a book about it but I remembered a friend of mine telling me – Anyone who writes a book must be a right big headed git, they must be up their own arse -, so I dismissed that idea and just walked past the youth hostel at Perranporth which is in a lovely location overlooking the sea, I wished I could stay there but I had Buddy with me, never mind, we stayed on a camp site near an air field just outside St Agnes.

We set of towards Porthtowan next day, I had left Buddy's back packs in my car, they were OK for carrying light food and making him look cute but the novelty and attention he was getting was wearing thin, they were made of canvas and got surprisingly heavy when it rained and I could see him struggling, so I ditched them and because I was now a bit fitter, I carried about a kilo of his emergency dried food in my bag. When we reached Portreath at about 4pm I gave him a full tin of dog food outside the shop and also got him another for later (I paid for this one by the way) and a litre of water for me, I wanted to wild camp and my map showed no streams ahead from which I could filter water.

Because I had water this time, I didn't have to wild camp in a valley which is where most streams are usually found, I could camp anywhere. I came across a small flat piece of grass right next to the path, it was high up about 10 yards away from the cliff edge. It had the most fantastic view from my tent door towards St Ives, I had to pinch myself because of the stunning sea views, the only problem was if the wind got up and changed direction, if I didn't peg my tent down properly we'd be off like a kite over the cliff and I am no good at flying. I phoned my sister and described where I was and what I was doing, she was shocked and said I was mad. Well it was a bit mad when you think about it, anything could have happened, a mad axe man, extreme weather or my worst fear, me sleep walking out of my tent and over the cliff never to be seen again.

The walking was flat and easy next day as I headed towards St Ives via Godrevy point where there is a car park very near the edge of the cliff. I passed a couple who had set up a table and chairs complete with a table cloth at the cliff edge, they had a spectacular view. They were sat there at the table having lunch like it was the most natural thing in the world. Their view of Gwithian beach and St Ives was unbelievable, I thought I must remember this spot and come back and do the same one day.

After any wild camp, as all good campers know, you carry away any rubbish, the saying goes - Take only photographs and leave only footprints – so with this in mind, I was still carrying my rubbish from last nights camp. I had been promising myself a full English breakfast, so when I reached the cafe at Red River, I put my small bag of rubbish and the empty water bottle in the bin in the ladies toilet. I went into the cafe and was just about to order my food when I felt a tap on my shoulder. It was the owner and in his hand was my rubbish that he had retrieved out of the bin in the ladies. In front of all the other customers in the cafe, he told me, with some venom, to take it away with me as I couldn't leave it in his bin, what a sad git! I was so embarrassed, I felt like some criminal, I have never been told off for putting rubbish in a bin before, what was his problem, everyone was staring at me! I wanted to say it wasn't mine but he had obviously spotted me walking in with it, I was in half a mind to not give him my custom and walk away but why cut off your nose to spite your face, there was nowhere else to eat and I was starving. So I reluctantly took my rubbish back from this twit and took it outside and put it back in my rucksack. I went back in and found I had missed breakfast as it was now 12.05pm. I hid my annoyance as I asked for a sausage and egg sandwich and a pot of tea. Me and Buddy shared it sat outside as I seethed with anger. I will go back there one day and get my revenge, I had no choice that day but to do as he said, the little Hitler, I am sure he could have handled it a little more diplomatically, he could have asked me politely away from other customers but he didn't, it was like he purposely wanted to show me up in front of everyone. I deposited my rubbish in the next bin on the beach and was annoyed all the way to St Ives. I know it was such a small thing to get upset about but you can't help yourself when you are tired.

There were plenty of camp sites and chalets behind the sand dunes on Gwithian beach, I had a quick look at one site but it announced at the entrance – ABSOLUTEY NO DOGS ALLOWED EVER ON THIS SITE GO AWAY ALL DOG OWNERS AND THEIR FURRY FOUR LEGGED MUTTS! Well that's a bit of an exaggeration but you get the gist. So even though I was again tired and it was only 1pm, I was wishing I could stop for the day and put my feet up, but something inside me made me push on, was it that little thought of getting to Poole?

We walked on, past some shops where Buddy got another tin and the young female shop assistant was enthralled at the fact that Buddy and I were backpacking together, I could see the envy in her eyes, she was stuck there in the shop, working, a virtual prisoner, but I was reeling in the fact that I was free as a bird, if not a bit smelly and knackered.

We pushed on to the next camp site marked on my map, it was behind the lovely Carbis Bay beach. I was in dire need of a shower again and some decent food. I walked up the main road looking for the site but couldn't find it. I stopped a man who was obviously a local and asked him if he knew where it was, he didn't know. I showed him my map and he scratched his head and said "Yes it should be here love, like you say but I have lived here 3 years and I have never seen a camp site here, do you mean the one two miles inland up the main road or the one just past St Ives?" I answered "No, I mean the one that should be right here where my map says it should be". He shrugged his shoulders and walked away towards his nice cosy house and left me and Buddy standing there reading my map and trying to work out what to do. A young couple passed us and I asked them did they know where the camp site was, they pointed behind me, I turned around and looked to where they were pointing, I was confused because they were pointing at a giant Tescos store! They told me Tescos had bought the camp site land 3 years ago and that is where the site used to be!

I had had enough of walking for today and the last thing I wanted was to walk miles inland or even more miles up the path to the one past St Ives, that one, for all I knew could also now have a bloody Tescos built on it. It was decision time again. I thought if you can't beat 'em join 'em, I decided I may as well get some shopping at Tescos (a sign of Tescos success perhaps, if it's there - shop in it!) and then look for a B & B. I loaded two plastic bags with food and beer, strapped my walking sticks to my rucksack and walked up the road, one heavy bag in each hand and a heavy backpack on my back, knocking on B & B doors asking for a room, not necessarily with a view but one that took dogs.

I wasn't very successful. None of them took dogs or were full if they did. I was getting worried and was getting that homeless tramp feeling again, I was starting to panic. I was walking slower because of the weight of the three bags and was telling myself off for buying heavy cans of beer. I was frustrated because I was walking in the wrong direction and wasting time and energy again looking for accommodation! I had walked about a mile up the main road when one kind gentleman directed me to the inland camp site that he assured me was still open.

I trudged on cursing myself and Tescos, it was dark when I found the site, the office was closed and the site was very quiet. There was a telephone number on the reception door and when I phoned him, the owner told me I could camp and pay in the morning. Brilliant, I was saved by the bell, I set up camp, sorted Buddy and I out with food, had a long shower in their sparkly new shower block, then while Buddy slept in the tent, I took a can of beer into the laundry room which was luckily still open and did a load of laundry whilst sat in the warm supping my beer, it was luxury, talk about small things amusing small minds!

When it was time to set off next day, I went to the office to pay but it was still closed and there was no sign of anyone, I know it was wrong, I could have posted some money through the letterbox, but I didn't, honest mister, I only had fifty pound notes so I just walked away towards Carbis Bay. I will go back there one day, honestly, and stay there again and pay for an extra night, it was a nice camp site and I don't know what I would have done if I hadn't found it.

Two miles later and back on the path, I was finding it hard not to pass the first cafe we came to. I ordered two crumpets and a pot of tea, only because I had a craving for butter for some reason. The cafe had a veranda overlooking the sea with a beautiful view of St Ives, but alas, no dogs were allowed on it, so I sat around the back looking at the dustbins but appreciating the fact that I was sat on a chair. The crumpets were soon devoured washed down with plenty of tea, I take two sugars in my cup and I was finding that having a full pot of tea to myself meant I was having eight sugars! Bloody hell! I set of again full of butter, caffeine and sugar, the weather was glorious, not only was I full of food but I was also full of the joys of spring even though it was September. The butter, caffeine, sugar and weather was giving me some sort of high, like I was on drugs! The world was wonderful, I was clean and had a full belly, I was once again in my element as I walked into St Ives.

The light in St Ives is definitely different, that's why lots of artists live here and this day was no exception, the sea, sky and sand were so bright! It was like I was walking in a watercolour. People were just sat around admiring the view. I stopped and took my backpack off to listen to a bloke telling stories to a crowd of people in the open air and when some musicians started playing classical music I thought bugger it, I am in no rush, so I sat down for a while and listened to the lovely violin and cello. For a moment I wished I was just a normal tourist and could just sit here all day and listen but I was on a mission, I was a backpacker who wanted to walk as much of the South West Coast Path as possible, so

I reluctantly set off again, past the Tate Gallery and round St Ives Head.

The next bit of the path towards Zennor is supposedly one of the hardest bit on the north coast, to me it wasn't any different from what I had already done, it had all been bloody hard carrying a bloody heavy rucksack. There was no accommodation for 20 miles but I wasn't worried, I was self sufficient and knew I could wild camp. I found my two sticks came in handy as I stumbled over the rocky path leading to Zennor. When I got there, because of all my dawdling, it was time to camp again and I had only done 7 miles!

I found the only bit of flat ground that was big enough to pitch my tent after a bit of clearing away of rocks and brambles. It was near a bridge over a river, my green tent was almost camouflaged amongst the ferns. I had pitched the tent and was cooking my noodles when a couple stopped on the bridge and started chatting. They were backpacking too, walking the other way and were looking for a flat spot for their tent, they were walking from Land's End to St Ives for a week. They asked me all sorts of questions about my kit and were very impressed I was backpacking with a dog. When they asked was I doing the whole path I answered "maybe", I didn't want to say yes any more, I didn't want to tempt fate, but deep down I knew I was going to try to get to Poole. They asked did I have a blog or a web site and was I doing it for charity. I answered no to all, I would have a blog if only I knew what one was. They wished me luck and walked on looking for a flat camping spot, which I knew they would struggle to find because I hadn't passed any. They had said they were envious of me for being able to even attempt the whole path. Again, I was feeling very proud of myself as I got into my tent, so much so, I don't know how I got my head through the tent door that night, I was becoming a right big head.

CHAPTER 8
Why Stop Now ?

There was a very heavy dew overnight and everything was damp. The tent was wet inside and out, wetter and heavier than if it had rained. The uncut grass on the path, wet through with dew, soon soaked my supposed waterproof boots. I was going to have wet socks all day, lovely! It was tough going, we walked past Pendeen Watch, a big white lighthouse that is so popular with tourists that there is an ice cream van parked outside. Of course I couldn't pass without buying one. I sat in the shade of a wall with my feet in the sun to dry them off and ate my ice cream while I read my map. It indicated a camp site about half a mile inland from the path at a place called Botallack. There was a pub near it. Whoopee!

In the camp site shop I asked for dog food, they had none, only corned beef, so Buddy not only thought it was his birthday, but he thought Christmas had come early as well as he wolfed down a full tin. I washed and showered, then went to the pub with him. I stuffed myself with food and beer and asked the landlord did he have any dog food to sell me. He gave me a sad look then told me he'd had to have his dog put down last week so no, he didn't have any. I was sorry I had asked, talk about bad timing!

I was getting used to sitting in public places, eating and drinking, sat there on my own, I didn't give a hoot. You wouldn't believe it but when I was young I was extremely shy, if anyone just looked at me I would go bright red. Here I was, sat in this pub full of independence. Look at me now! Well I prefer it if you didn't but at least if you did I wouldn't go red with embarrassment.

I chatted to a couple of rock climbers from the Lake District about the local climbs around Cornwall, they came down here this time every year and always had nice weather. They asked me what I was up to and when I told them they were very impressed and asked was I going to walk around Portland as it was a new addition to the South West Coast Path. I didn't know what Portland was and tried to hide my ignorance. I had up to now purposely made a habit of not looking too far ahead in the map books because it was too daunting looking at all the miles I still had to walk. So I didn't know about this Island of Portland, I just said to them that if it was attached to the mainland, then I would have to walk around it, otherwise it didn't count.

There was a beer tent outside selling real ale and burgers. A comedian was telling jokes and singing, he told a tale of getting drunk on J2O (jay two O) which is an orange soft drink, by adding loads of vodka to it and calling it a J20% (jay 20 percent) I thought it was funny, but I had drunk two pints of beer. I sat on a bench and watched him for a while enjoying the warm evening, pint of the black stuff in hand. I had put clean dry socks on, I twiddled my toes - life was perfect!

Next day with the sun shining, I packed up the tent and walked back to the coast, yesterday I had walked past the Levant Mine, an old tin mine that's been restored. It's steam engine still steams but only on Wednesdays when it shows itself off to the public. Today I took some photos of the area with my phone camera not knowing the pictures I was taking were useless, I didn't find out until I got home!

I was within a days walk from Land's End - my original goal - there was no way I was going to stop the walk there, I was enjoying myself too much. I still had no time restraints, I wasn't spending much money and Buddy and I were fit and healthy, why stop now?

We walked past Cape Cornwall, a rather grand name for a little bit of land sticking out to sea but apparently it's called a Cape because that's where two different seas meet and in the olden days, it was thought to be Land's End but now we know it's not. On towards Senna Cove where a red tap on my map indicated a fresh water supply at the public toilets. I know it doesn't sound much but by now water had become like liquid silver, it was hard to get and very precious. I had been umpteen times to Sennen Cove when me and Tony came and based ourselves at Buryan, a small village further inland, so now I just headed for the tap at Sennen, it was luxury not having to filter water and just fill my bottles with tap water. It was a hot day and the place was crowded with tourists. I replenished mine and Buddy's food supplies as there was nothing ahead but wilderness and tonight was another wild camp night.

I slowly trudged with my heavy pack amongst the tourists, glad I'd had a shower last night and not having to walk downwind of everybody. People were still walking faster than me, I felt like a snail as I walked uphill out of Sennen Cove and towards Land's End. I think people have cottoned on to the fact that if you park either side of Land's End and walk in, you don't have pay to get in to see it, hoards of people were walking my way towards the most westerly point in Britain.

At Land's End I did not stop to admire the view, it was too crowded and I had been here twice before anyway, I just admired the view as I walked on past the very end of this land we call Britain. You are not allowed to walk right to the very end where the rocks meet the sea any more, I came here about 5 years ago when you were still allowed and was very disappointed as the views were stunning but the area stunk of stale pee (or urine if you are posh)!

I left the crowds behind having pictures taken at the famous sign post and carried on. I knew there was a camp site further on at Treen, I knew this area well, but why rush, I fancied a wild camp on the edge of Britain, I may never get this chance again, to be able to set up my tent overlooking the Longships Lighthouse, with just me, Buddy and peace and quiet.

I found a natural spring about a mile on, water coming out of the ground as clear as bottled water. I pitched the tent near it away from the path on soft bouncy grass. I was going to have a nice comfy bed tonight. It was still early, about 4pm, I just lay there in the doorway of the tent on my blow up matt, my head on my rucksack and looked at the view and some sort of falcon feeding it's chicks on the cliffs for an hour or so until I got hungry, it was glorious not having to move.

I had not only reached my goal but had passed it, I was pleased to be able to carry on. Everything was going right, the weather especially. I was still taking it one day at a time, just to see how far I could get, don't tempt fate by thinking of the end at Poole, because my favourite saying is "If you want to make God laugh – tell him your plans"

We both slept for another 12 hours, still more sleeping than walking, it was a good job no one was watching, it was getting embarrassing. Buddy had a swim to cool down before we got to Porth Curno, I knew he wasn't allowed on the beach there, the sand is so clean and white I can understand why. This beach is one of the best ever and is overlooked by the classy Minack Theatre. Further on, I would have liked to have camped at Treen, one of my favourite spots in Cornwall but it was only 1pm when we got there so all we did was use their shop to get dog meat and some dinner for me. They only had that cheap dog food, the one that smells of fish and looks disgusting but Buddy didn't mind, his eyes were out on stalks again.

The next beach is my very favourite one and like a woman with a box of chocolates, I am keeping it to myself and not telling anyone where it is. We walked on past it towards Penberth Cove, a lovely unspoilt fishing village, but alas Buddy wasn't allowed to step paw on the beach or the village, he wasn't even allowed to walk through the car park! Like second hand (I mean class) citizens, we had to go all the way round while pulling at our flat caps.

By the time we reached the grandly named Lamorna, I was hungry again. I knew there was a cafe there that did cream teas. I was drooling as I rounded the corner as I approached, knowing my luck, it would be closed or out of clotted cream. But no – I had my first (and not last) cream tea. If you have never been to Cornwall or Devon you won't know what one is, it consists of a scone or two if you're lucky, jam and what I call, heart attack clotted cream, sometimes you get butter as well for good measure, and a pot of tea. Eight sugars and ten thousand calories later I was having a hot sweat! It was the best cream tea ever, it was almost orgasmic!

Rather than fill me with energy, sat down in the cafe, reading my map, I wanted to stop for the day, I'd had enough. There were no camp sites further up the path at Mousehole (pronounced Mowzul). I knew there was a camp site about 2 miles inland so I walked up the road to this very basic farm camp site, but at least it had a shower.

An old farmers wife opened the farm door and I asked could I camp, she said "Yes, that will be four pounds". I gave her a five pound note and she very quickly snapped it out of my hand and started feeling it?! She asked "Is it a fiver?" I answered "Yes it is". She disappeared into her front room and came out with a glass ashtray full of change, she handed it to me and asked me to find a pound coin, it was then I realised she was blind! I asked her did her shower take coins, she told me it took 20p coins so I got five 20's out, I could have took as much as I wanted, I could literally have robbed her blind, but of course I didn't, she was a lovely old lady, God bless her.

Even though it was a dairy farm, they had no milk so it was bloody noodles and powdered milk for tea again. Mine was the only tent in the field and it rained all night, it was a good job I was knackered, I was too tired to be miserable. In the morning the rain had stopped. I still had only got wet through twice while walking, which was amazing considering I had walked what I though was nearly 315 miles, half of the South West Coast Path.

Next day we walked into Mousehole and I had a disappointing pasty for brunch, it must have been yesterdays and was as hard as a brick, Buddy got most of it. Then at Newlyn I managed to go wrong and ended up on the beach at a dead end and had to retrace my steps and waste precious energy. I was cheered up when I saw a sign, it read :-

You will notice that this notice is not worth noticing.

It made me chuckle, some one has got a sense of humour. Onto Penzance where I got Buddy a kilo of dried dog food from a pet shop. The owner had a giant lizard parked on his shoulder. I wanted to tell him he was in Penzance and it should have been a parrot but he probably knew that and many a smart arse would have probably tried telling him that already so I said nowt and just paid for the food and left

We walked past St Michael's Mount a picturesque little island with a castle on it that you can walk to when the tide is out, or get on a little ferry to if it's in. Me and Tony had walked onto it only last year. This time I just waved as I walked past it, head down on a mission to find tonight's over night stop. I was heading for a camp site marked on my map, I'd better not say the name because the owner sold me some cans of beer and swore me to secrecy (he had no alcohol licence and I told him I was desperate for a beer). There was a takeaway as well so I got a big fat curry for my dinner.

The next stage of the walk goes round the Lizard Peninsula. I had walked it in four days last year with Tony as back up driver as practise, this time it was for real! So I had been here before and knew what was coming up. At Porthleven, a lovely place, I stocked up at the local shop. Buddy got his now usual tin there and then, so I didn't have to carry it (rather in him than on me). We walked over Loe Bar, a sand bar that separates a lake of fresh water from the sea. The weather was calm and I wanted to wild camp tonight so I was a little naughty and set up camp in a farmers field just before I reached Mullion, I'd filled my water bottles at a cafe after I'd ate my umpteenth ice cream.

At Mullion Cove the next day, I had breakfast in the little cafe there, I had what they called an economy breakfast, one of everything, one egg, one rasher of bacon, one sausage, toast and tea, it was delicious as well as great value and I told them so, they even let me take Buddy in as it had started drizzling outside.

It was easy going and when I reached Kynance Cove, I stopped to admire the lovely views and watch as a group of canoeists launched themselves into rough waves, they had to time it right or they would have been thrown by the waves and looked like right plonkers, they all made it and started paddling towards Lizard Point. As I walked I could look down from the cliffs and follow their progress, they canoed under rock arches and amongst the seals, I thought what a great way to see the coast line and wildlife.

There were more seals at Lizard Point, a great name, better than the one I saw in Scotland recently at the side of Loch Lommond – Ferkin Point – if you say it fast and put the words – what's the – in front, you will know what I mean. My favourite name is in Scotland also. It's an island on the west coast called the Isle of Ewe, say that fast and it comes out I Love You, what a great place to get married or engaged.

I would have loved to have camped outside the youth hostel at Lizard Point but they didn't open 'till 5pm and I didn't want to wait around to find I couldn't because I had a dog so I cracked on and walked past the Devils Frying Pan, another great name and on to the beautiful fishing village of Cadgwith. I was aiming for a camp site I had stayed at in my 'Bongo', a little camper van I had a few years ago. I loved that van but had to sell it because it cost too much to run. It had a rising roof, cooker, fridge and sink. This time at Kugger I was in a tent and I noticed how cold it was getting at night. I phoned Tony who owns a massive camper van and asked would he come down and join me to give me a bit of luxury. He said yes, he would come down but in his car! Never mind at least I tried.

We set off towards Coverack next day where I'd stayed last year at the youth hostel. This time I just used the shop to stock up, every shop, cafe, ice cream van and pasty shop was now really difficult to walk past, I just had to stop and use them.

Our next camp was a big disappointment, I walked a couple of miles out of the way to find the one at Porthkerris, it was not on my map but was signposted

towards the diving centre. It was just a field, the facilities were 1 mile down the road at sea level, was this a joke? Obviously they cater for people who have cars who drive down for a shower and a pee. I walked down and they let me pitch my tent near a run down building so I didn't have to keep walking two miles every time I needed the loo. The office closed shortly after they ripped me off for 8 quid and the showers took 50p's, I didn't have any 50p's so no shower tonight, I may as well have been wild camping, it was a cold, damp, miserable evening. The only bit I enjoyed was watching the divers disembark
from the diving boat, they had been out to dive around the Mannacle shipwrecks and had been looking for whales.

On to Pothhallow next day where there is a weather forecast board with a rock dangling on a peace of wire, the board reads:-

CONDITION.	FORECAST.
Stone is Wet	Rain
Stone is Dry	Not Raining
Shadow on Ground	Sunny
White on Top	Snowing
Can't see Stone	Foggy
Swinging Stone	Windy
Stone Jumping Up and Down	Earth Quake
Stone Gone	Tornado

I thought it was funny any way. The stone was dry today! I probably wouldn't have found it that funny if the stone was wet and swinging.

We headed for the Helford river and stopped at a cafe at Helford Point, I would like to say so I could get change for the ferry but no, I was starving again and had a delicious jacket potato with tuna and mayo. The owner asked me was I walking the whole path, I said yes, maybe. She asked was I walking it for charity and I said no, not knowing I could probably have got the food for free if I had said yes. She asked had I seen the half way marker at

Porthallow, I just said no because I hadn't. Deep down I was gutted, not because I hadn't noticed it but because I thought I had passed the half way point miles ago near Penzance, my rubbish calculations must have been wrong, I never was good at maths!

I had to change a £50 note in the cafe because there was a ferry to catch over the Helford river and I knew the ferryman wouldn't be too pleased if I handed him a £50 note for a £2 fare. I was dreading this ferry, I knew Buddy didn't like them and he went on strike as we approached the ferry point, he knew what was coming as I pulled him along by his lead. I had to swing open a semicircular black board to make a brightly coloured circle so the ferryman could see someone was hailing the ferry from across the river. It was a nervous five minute wait for poor old Buddy and when the boat arrived I had to drag him on. He screamed and barked all the way and I found myself apologising and lying again, saying sorry but the dog has never been on a ferry before.

The camp site on my map this time wasn't a Tesco's but had closed 3 years earlier and was now an equestrian centre and it took a lot of main road walking to find another, I was walking in circles again wasting time and energy. I must learn to   plan

                                                  a

                                                  h

                                                  e

                                                  a

                                                  d

CHAPTER 9
Joy of Joys

I phoned my mate Tony again, he said he couldn't come to meet me yet as he was busy doing something important but he would come soon. I was coming into Falmouth and to the end of my second map book. My other two books were still in the car at Crantock. I couldn't continue without a map so when I got into Falmouth I left my heavy bag and sticks at a local shop. The kind lady assistant put it behind the counter, she nearly pulled her back picking it up, she asked how the hell had I walked with that thing on my back all the way from Minehead, I lied and said "You just get used to it". She directed me to a book shop in the town and luckily they had a copy of the Falmouth to Exmouth map book. We walked back through the streets of Falmouth, it was busy with people shopping, it was great walking without my pack on. I bought an envelope and posted my Padstow to Falmouth book back home to avoid me carrying two books.

I had wanted Tony to come down not only for a bit of company, I had spent 30 or so days on my own and had started talking to myself, even worse, I'd started talking to Buddy, but Buddy never did answer back! I wanted a lift in Tony's car to avoid the next stage which wasn't walking but involved catching two bloody ferries. So I had no lift and to try to avoid the ferries I phoned a local taxi rank up and was shocked to find they would charge £85 to get me to the next stage on the coast path!

So I apologised to Buddy as I dragged him onto the large ferry at Falmouth docks, he instantly started barking and crying. Luckily the ship had a toilet down below, so I took him in there and locked the door and pretended to use the loo, this seemed to shut him up so I stayed in there the whole time. Not only did I miss all the lovely views as it had no window but nobody else could use the loo! The journey took a long 20 minutes, I have never sat on a toilet holding a dog on a lead for that long before, I got some strange looks as I came out when the ship landed at St Mawes.

One down, one more to go. I had a disappointing cup of coffee at a cafe while waiting for the next ferry. It tasted horrible, like that cheap coffee you get from cheap supermarkets, like the cola that tastes like chicken, this coffee smelt of tuna fish of all things! I drank it anyway as it had 18 sugars in it.

The next ferry was one of those that Buddy really hates! The ones with the outboard motors are his worst nightmare especially when they go into reverse thrust, it's the noise and the vibration that upsets him. He screamed all the way and I once again found myself apologising to fellow passengers, this time I didn't lie because I knew they had seen me and him on the other ferry so I couldn't make excuses and say it was his first one. The ferryman told me in between screams that he had seen worse, one dog was so scared of his boat the owner just let his dog swim behind it. It was a short 5 minute journey and Buddy soon got over himself and we carried on, me with my brand new map book in hand feeling very proud of myself for getting over those hurdles and saving 85 quid in taxi fares.

The way I saw it, I had done two books (169 + 169 = 338 miles) I had one more 169 miles book and then the final one which was only 117 (169 + 117 = 286 miles) so only 286 miles to go -
could I possibly manage it and do all of the 630 miles of the South West Coast Path?

We landed at a place called Place which is a bit confusing but I'd been here before on one of my many expeditions when based at Crantock. I was hoping the camp site guy there didn't mind the fact that my car was still parked in his field, I hoped Tony would come down to meet me soon so we could go and pick it up.

By the time we had set off again and had calmed down after the ferry trips it was 5pm and we'd only done 3 miles of walking, this must be a record even for me, the fewest miles walked in a day but I felt like I'd achieved a lot and saved a fortune and not had to rely on Tony or anyone for assistance, in fact I didn't give a monkey's that I'd only done so few miles, I felt great, I was well into the swing of this backpacking lark and the sun had shone all day, I felt like everything was going right, the stress of going slowly had gone, the only thing now worrying me was the length of time I had left my car at Crantock, the owner must have thought I was taking the mickey.

There was a camp site marked on my map but I fancied a wild camp again as I'd had a lovely shower last night. I found a great spot near some toilets with a drinking water tap outside, I won't say where it was as it was on National Trust land and I don't want to spoil it for fellow backpackers. It was near a beach and as Buddy slept soundly, after dinner, I went and watched the moon shine on the sea, sat on a sand dune, the evening was warm. Bats flew around me and past the full moon. It was one of those special moments in time that you never forget.

It was 18th September and we must have been in the middle of an Indian Summer, I'd been counting the days since it had last rained while I was walking, it had rained a few times while I was in the tent in the evenings, but it had been dry during the day since I'd left Crantock two weeks ago. I knew I was lucky and I wasn't taking it for granted. It would soon be autumn! Would I make it to the end before it started snowing! I told myself to stop panicking at my still slow pace.

I knew I'd been lucky with the weather up to now, but I had this dread that as soon as Tony came down to meet me, the weather would change, it usually does, I don't know how he does it but bad weather always seems to follow him, I have witnessed it too many times for it to be a coincidence.

Next day we walked towards Portloe one of my favourite places, the walking and views were fantastic. By the time we got there I was craving a cream tea. This all sounds very jolly and I may be making this walking sound very easy which it wasn't, that's why I wanted calories all the time. The only place to get one was a posh hotel. I was again smelly after last nights wild camp and today's hot and sweaty walking. Thankfully they had an outside veranda where Buddy and I could sit downwind of the posh hotel clients. But I still had to go inside to order and the staff looked down their noses at me as I ordered a cream tea. I don't think they approved of muddy smelly walkers coming into their hotel. For that reason I thought sod it, on the way back to the veranda I picked up one of the hotels newspapers and like some cheeky tramp, I sat reading it waiting for my tray to arrive. It was delivered by a waiter in a smart suit on a sliver tray with the thickest, biggest white cotton serviette, it was big enough for me to use as a towel. I didn't have a towel with me to save on weight. I looked at this beautifully soft white peace of cloth and considered stealing it but decided against it but nearly changed my mind when they charged me a whopping £7.50 for one cream tea! I didn't have enough change on me and had to use my card. That'll teach me I thought as I choked on my tea! (I did nick a load of sugar though!)

Further down the path at East Portholland where the sea is just yards away from the houses, they have shutters on the doors and windows to keep the sea out. I met some Dutch men and their vintage cars. They had driven here on a vintage car rally to Land's End to take pictures of their prized cars with a backdrop of crashing waves. One very dashing young man started chatting (I'd like to say me up but I wasn't sure), I was sat on a bench having a rest and felt too dirty and smelly to chat him up. He seemed quite interested in what I was doing, he spoke good English and asked was I walking on my own, when I replied "No I am walking with my dog" and pointed at Buddy who was cocking his leg up and having a wee on his shiny well polished wheel, I could tell he wasn't amused but his mates thought it was funny. They all quickly got into their cars and rallied off into the distance.

It was again time to find a camping spot, I needed a shower but the nearest site was inland again up what looked like a cliff, I didn't have the energy to walk up hill so reluctantly I found a spot, again next to some loo's and a cafe that said it opened at 10am. The moon shone again over the sea when it went dark, everything seemed in black and white. I wished I could take a photo but knew it wouldn't turn out so I took a short video with my ipod but when I got home I accidentally deleted it like a plonker.

The next day dawned misty and cool, I didn't want to get out of my warm bed and fell back to sleep and stalled waiting for the cafe to open. I packed up just in time to see the shutters go up and I ordered a bacon sandwich and a mug of tea or a large cup as they call it down there.

The day was damp but no rain as we walked towards Mevagissey, through a field of intimidating looking cows, calves and the biggest bull I have ever seen the ring through its nose made it look worse. I made the biggest B line past them, it's a problem on your own going into fields with livestock in them, with a dog you can feel their anger and I knew I couldn't run fast if they decided to charge; I couldn't walk fast never mind run.

I headed for a camp site on my map that was right on the path, a much needed shower would be nice. As we walked downhill towards it at around 4pm, I had a good view of the whole site, there were tents erected but there was an absence of dogs. I found out why at the entrance, a sign read- NO DOGS-   so another clanger was heard being dropped. There was no way I could go another night and another long sweaty day without a shower, I was desperate, I panicked and asked the young receptionist was there any other sites nearby. She looked at my map and I noticed she was reading it upside down so my confidence in her instantly vanished. She told me they had a sister site that did take dogs and it was ' just around the corner '. I tried to get a second opinion as I wasn't sure she knew what she was taking about. I asked the guy in the takeaway who was serving a kid who couldn't decided which flavour drink he wanted, I interrupted and asked for directions, he said "Sorry I am very busy at the moment, ask the receptionist", so I gave up and started walking following her directions. An hour later I ended up at The Hanging Gardens of Heligan camp site, I was furious with her and myself, I was once again wasting time and energy looking for a shower but it was my own fault. It was dark and I was nearly in tears when I knocked on the door of the closed reception, tears of anger for not doing any planning, it's a good job Tony wasn't with me, he would have gone mad!

The kind deputy wardens came to my rescue and though the shop was shut they gave me some beans and eggs from their own kitchen and some food for Buddy which again made me feel very humble and for which I was truly thankful. They even opened up the laundrette especially for me, what lovely people they were. I put my tent up and fed Buddy then found I had no tin opener to open the beans. I asked the chap in the next caravan and he opened it for me and told me that heavy rain was forecast at any moment. But the best bit was still to come, in the toilet block, next to the laundrette, I found a bath! Joy of Joys! So as my clothes dried in the drier and Buddy was tucked up in bed, I had the most luxurious soak, it was fantastic.

It absolutely peed it down during the night which caused local flooding. Luckily the grass my tent was on was well drained. We woke up and every thing was damp so I put my sleeping bag in the drier for while. After a dinner last night of beans heated up in the tent awning because it was raining so hard outside and then again for breakfast with an added boiled egg, I set off back to the coast path like Nelly the Elephant, I'd packed my trunk and went trumperty trump – trump – trump – trump all the way there. These added miles worked out well worth it due to the warden's kindness and that great bath.

We reached Charlestown near St Austell where in the harbour, tall ships are docked and they are a huge tourist attraction. I wanted my picture taken here with Buddy but there was no one about to take it. I felt for the first time like Billynomates and very alone but only for a second, then a man appeared and took one of Buddy and I with a tall ship behind us.

I knew there was a camp site at Par Sands because I had been there years earlier but wasn't impressed because of the factory billowing out smoke next to it. This time I didn't give a monkey's if a nuclear power station was next to it, I wanted the comfort of a real camp site where there's usually a shop and beer and luxuries. This time it wasn't dogs that were the problem, this time they didn't allow tents! It was just a caravan site. I ended up camping further on, near yet another toilet block amongst some trees. It was a bit public as lots of dog walkers used it to walk their dogs. I lay down in the tent enjoying having a rest until it got dark, the owners didn't know I was in there, many a time I heard the sound of dog pee hitting the corners of my tent but I could do nothing about it as I was camping illegally, their owners shouting "Get away Fido", "Come here Bruno, No!".

　　We walked through the lovely fishing village of Polkerris next morning, then around Gribbin Head and onto Fowey (pronounced 'Foy') where I knew we had to catch yet another ferry. It was about 11am when we reached the ferry point, so I stalled a little here and went for a pot of tea in a tapas bar. I sat there listening to the weirdest music I have ever heard and drank my tea along with the delicious complementary fudge cake that came with it. I was putting off the inevitable ferry journey, it was only a short one but it was the one that had given Buddy his ferry phobia last year.

　　I lied and apologised to the man in brown corduroy pants who was sat next to me on the boat as Buddy sung his ferry song, I thought what a snob as this man disembarked and said he'd enjoyed the floor show, what a stuck up git he was!

　　If I was to recommend any day walk to anyone, this is the one, Polruan to Polperro, it's lovely scenery but with lots of steps and climbs which the South West Coast Path has in abundance, if all the steps were put together on the South West Coast Path, I reckon they would make a stairway to heaven – really, there are that many of them and they seem to be built for people with six foot long legs. There was a luxury yacht anchored in Lantic Bay, the occupants were having lunch on deck, what a life!

We walked past Watch House Cove where apparently Daphne Du Maurier wrote some of her books in the hide out she had there. As I walked past, it felt like she was walking with us, it was a bit spooky, the hairs on the back of my neck stood up, she walked with us until we reached a gate and I left her there, I thought, "I really have been on my own too long, I must ring Tony!"

At Polperro the first camp site I came to no longer existed, the other was a mile inland up the steepest of roads, I was so knackered by now, the thought of walking up it made me decide to shell out and book in a B & B. After knocking on many doors to find they were all full, I managed to cadge a lift from a lovely Welsh bloke who kindly gave Buddy and I a lift in his truck, me in the front and Bud in the back. We camped at Great Kellow Farm, at least the walk back to the path would be downhill tomorrow.

I rang Tony last night and he'd finally decided to come down and do some walking with us. I'd be glad of the company, I'd been walking 42 days now on my own, not that I was counting, but it seemed like forever, it was taking so long to walk this path my hair had grown two inches! Would I finish before it turned grey? I still had a long way to go and I stopped myself from thinking about it because it made me panic. Tony would help, it would break it up a bit, I could go light weight for a while, I could go get my car, but best of all we could avoid any ferries because we would have two cars between us. He agreed to meet me in Plymouth in a couple of days time, I for once, looked ahead in the map book and there was only one more ferry ride between here and Plymouth.

It was a hot day as we walked between Polperro and Looe and the going was tough after that. I found a camp site that was signposted from the road at about 5pm. It was just up the side road at a place I won't name. I knocked on the reception door that had a sign on it "Hot Food and Cold Beer Served Here" which is a sight for sore eyes for a backpacker. A young guy answered the door and I asked him could I camp for the night, he said "Are you aware that this is a naturist site", thinking I would get a laugh out of him, I said" No, but does that mean I have to take my clothes off?" He never batted an eyelid and just said "No, but we do allow overnight backpackers to camp here" I paid him the £10 fee and told him I would be in the bar later for food and drink. I'd just put my tent up when this elderly gent who looked just like grandad on Only Fools and Horses knocked on the reception door, he was carrying a huge heavy rucksack that towered over his head. I overheard him also ask could he camp the night and I heard exactly the same question "Are you aware this is a naturist site?" Grandad came up with some funny remark to which the young guy still stayed very pan faced, he'd probably heard it all before poor bloke.

Grandad put his tent up next to mine. He grunted every time he bent down, I could tell he was knackered. He told me in the bar later that he had just set off from Plymouth and was doing a week's walk towards Megavissy. He had got off the train that morning and his bag was too heavy. I could see why next morning when I saw him sat on a chair he'd carried from Plymouth, his tent was huge as well, fancy carrying your own chair, no wonder his bag was heavy.

The sun hadn't quite come up at 9am as the site was in a deep valley. I thought the occupants of the nudist camp were being polite as they walked around next morning with big thick housecoats on, they went about washing up and getting water for their caravans or they sat about drinking tea. Grandad had already packed up and gone, I was packing my tent away when the sun suddenly appeared from behind the hill, it was still very strong and it soon warmed up. To my horror, the housecoats started coming off and the nudist's bits and bobs appeared, they weren't being polite at all, they were just waiting for the sun to appear. I tried desperately to pack up more quickly as one man walked past me to the bins with the smallest bit of rubbish in his hand wearing nothing but flip flops. I tried not to look but he did have a nice bum. The litter in his hand was just an excuse to walk past me and show off his wedding tackle. On the way back to his caravan he paused to talk to me and asked me what I was up to. I couldn't concentrate on what I was saying or doing because I couldn't help but notice how white his willy was, the rest of his body was brown and tanned, he must put sun cream on it I thought as I tried to continue our conversation. He walked off and his flip flops weren't the only thing that was flipping and flopping.

I set off again towards Whitsand Bay thinking I'd seen it all now. I packed in early to leave a decent days walk for tomorrow into Plymouth. The sun was still hot as I set up camp in a large commercial camp site that had swimming pools, shops and pubs. I was lying in the sunshine near my tent enjoying myself when this male backpacker rolled up and pitched his tent next to mine. He started chatting and told me his name was Peter and my reputation had preceded me, he had heard of a woman walking the coast path on her own with a dog! Bloody hell, I was becoming famous! People had been passing him and telling him about this strange woman with a dog walking the path and he'd finally caught up with me. He told me he had been ' bombing' it from Minehead and had been doing an average of twenty miles a day starting sometimes at 5.30am.

He wasn't the kind of person I would normally talk to. He was a little eccentric and swayed from side to side as he talked, he even did it in the pub later when he was sat down, but we both had one thing in common, well two really, we were both doing the same walk and we both liked talking about our kit. He told me he'd walked to here in super fast time and I was jealous and lied again about how long I'd been walking because it was so embarrassing how long it had taken me to get this far. He bragged as he talked of how fast he walked, when he told me he'd been chucked out of the Ramblers Association because he walked so fast, I stopped listening. He kept on talking about his wife, they had recently split up and he was still in love with her I think, I stopped listening again. Later he told me he was catching the train home at Plymouth, I asked him, as he was so close to the end and the finish, why wasn't he going to Poole, he told me he didn't fancy walking in October and bad weather and there was a firing range coming up that he said wasn't open and needed a 30 mile detour inland. I was shocked to hear this I knew nothing of this firing range as it was in my other book that was in the car.

I waited 'till he packed up next morning as I didn't fancy walking with him, not because I didn't like him but I didn't want to have to walk fast to keep up with him. Off he went, Buddy and I set off at our normal slow pace. So I was very surprised when I caught up with him at the headland at Rame Head and then again at Kingsand. We ended up walking together and chatted along the way, he told me he was a chess champion, well that explained a lot, he was retired and didn't own a television, Billy Connelly the comedian once said "Never trust a man when left in a room on his own with a tea cosy, doesn't put it on his head!" Well I am the same with anyone who doesn't own a TV, it's not that I don't trust them , I just think it's kinda odd.

We shared a cream tea at a cafe in a park near Cremyll where the ferry point is, it was here he admitted that because he had walked so fast and pushed himself too much, he had injured his leg and that's why he was going home, he couldn't continue to the end even if he wanted to. This made me feel quite smug and it sort of justified me taking my time and not rushing, it was the typical hare and tortoise situation, this revelation cheered me up no end or was it the cream tea?

I warned him about Buddy's phobia as we approached the ferry, he said "Don't worry I'll pretend I don't know you". It was a large ship but it had no toilet to hide in but was big enough to walk around so when Buddy kicked off I just walked around the deck which seemed to keep him quiet but as soon as I stopped walking he started again. We must have walked around the bloody thing about 20 times before it docked at Stonehouse in Plymouth. Again I saw no views nor did I have the chance to sit down for a rest, I got some funny looks, mad dog and even madder woman on board! Peter thought it was very amusing.

We knocked on doors along the path through the town looking for a B & B that took dogs and didn't charge too much, we found one they had two spare rooms, Buddy's second B & B. After a shower and rest all three of us went out for something to eat, what a treat and a change from bloody noodles. We went to a back street chippy to avoid paying restaurant prices and sat and stuffed ourselves then sat outside a pub under one of those canvas awnings next to a heater and had a few pints, I don't think he was much of a drinker, he only drank shandy. We were next to the marina, it was a warm evening, Buddy was asleep at my feet, a guy with a guitar sat singing, the place was full of people enjoying their holiday and the Indian summer, I felt great.

I phoned Tony and gave him the address of my B & B, he drove down overnight and met up   with us at breakfast. The landlady kindly gave him breakfast for free. Peter went to catch his train home and me, Tony and Buddy drove off to find somewhere to base ourselves for a week. My prediction for Tony bringing bad weather was correct, there were a few storms on the way for the week ahead so we decided not to camp but to go find a static caravan somewhere on the path between Plymouth and Exeter.

All the vans were full near the coast but this was no problem as we had transport. We booked into one a few miles inland near Burgh Island it was going to be luxury having a real bed for a while and being able to go lightweight. I spread all my smelly kit out in one of the many bedrooms to air out and the next day we drove to Crantock to pick my car up. The owner wasn't there so I posted a thank you note through his door along with a £20 note for his next chippy run for him and his staff.

Next day, Tony drove us to Plymouth and we walked from the point where I had finished. Of all the 630 miles of the beautiful coast path, Tony picked the worst bit, it was built up, industrial and the docks stank, the scenery wasn't exactly worth writing home about. He left us as planned and walked back to his car while Buddy and I walked on towards the river Yealm where he had

89

arranged to pick us up. I was back walking with a light day sack on, absolutely brilliant.

There's another ferry crossing at the river Yealm but because Tony was with us we didn't have to take it which was a good job as it had stopped running for the season. Back at the caravan I wallowed in the comfort of a bed, heating, a TV and great food and beer.

We parked my car near Burgh Island next day and Tony's car at the other side of the Yealm ferry point. We walked from car to car Tony had a more enjoyable walk this time. We had to cross the river Erme today but no ferry was needed here, you had to time it right and know what time low tide was, Tony worked this out by buying a tide book. At low tide it is possible to wade across, it involves taking your shoes and socks off and rolling your trousers up. Tony very rarely take his shoes and socks off even when he goes indoors, he has trampled dog shit into peoples houses on many occasions, so when he rolled his trousers up to wade the river, I saw his milk bottle white legs, I don't think they have ever seen the sun, it was a sight for sore eyes.

We reached my car and to my horror, found that I had left the lights on, the battery was as flat as a pancake. We had no phone signal to ring the AA, I prepared myself for Tony to explode and start shouting at me for being so stupid but surprisingly he didn't. A nice man in a white van happened to have some jump leads and got us going, panic over. We collected the other car and drove back to our luxury caravan.

The predicted storms arrived, I blamed it on Tony but at least I wasn't camping. I soon found out Tony is a fair weather walker, he refused to walk next day as it was peeing it down. He dropped me off at Bantham, another out of season ferry was avoided here and it is recommend you don't try and wade the river Avon at low tide because it's too dangerous, so Tony saved me a 9 miles inland walk.

It rained all day and everything got wet but it was easy going with a light pack and I knew I could dry out at the end of the day, I didn't know it at the time but I very nearly didn't see the end of the day!

CHAPTER 10
Summit Fever

We had said we would meet up at Salcombe, Tony parked his car there and walked towards us, we met at Sharp Tor where the path is cut into the rock and there are beautiful views over Salcombe Harbour. We started walking back together and had just got to Splatcove Point (an appropriate name as I was soon to find out) Buddy was ahead of us sniffing everything as usual when just around the corner we heard a loud crack. We all instantly froze. It had been raining heavily all day so I thought it was an avalanche or a landslip or something, then a loud crunch and then a car alarm going off. We walked a few yards round the corner to find a huge tree had landed on a car and was now blocking the way. If we had been a couple seconds earlier, we would all have been under it. The car was all crumpled, the windscreen smashed, the windscreen wipers stuck up through the branches. With the alarm going off Tony knocked on the nearest house but no one answered so we had to climb over it all to get to Salcombe, it was a near miss, but I suppose if you are going to die it's better being hit by a falling tree on a lovely walk than being run over by a number 9 bus.

We parked the two cars up again next day and I was paranoid about leaving the headlights on again. We put one at East Portlemouth and one at Torcross, saving another ferry crossing. We walked in lovely weather making good progress, even Tony was knackered at the end of the day, I think he was shocked by how hard the going was with all the ups and downs, I told him he should try it with a heavy back pack on.

The weather was again bad next day so Tony, the fair weather walker, dropped me off at yesterdays finish point and arranged to pick me up at Dartmouth. The boots I had worn up to now were worn out and leaked like a sieve when it rained so I swapped them with a spare pair I had in my car, hopefully they would keep my feet a bit drier and today was the day to test them. Buddy and I walked together over Slapton Sands and past the beautiful looking but commonly named Blackpool Sands. When I saw it from a distance it was very picturesque and I though I will definitely come back here one day when I have more time, but when I descended to the beach a big notice said - NO DOGS ON THIS BEACH EVER! - so I changed my mind.

Tony picked me up at Dartmouth. Overnight we discussed the possibility of me walking to Poole and finishing the whole walk, it was now 1st of October. We or rather I, decided it would make life easier for me if I was on my own without Buddy, it had been difficult finding accommodation with a dog so Tony agreed to take him home with him when he left. He also lent me £500 so I had no money worries and could use more B & B's or Youth Hostels if the weather stayed bad. I was determined now to get to Poole, I had summit fever! I was going to get there even if I had to crawl!

I have always been the same, when I get my teeth into something, I won't let go, like a dog with a bone. I have always been a stubborn git with a fierce determination. Like the time the infant school bully followed me home from school one day, why she did, I don't know, I must have annoyed her or something, or maybe because I was the smallest squirt in school and I was easy prey. I was minding my own business walking home when she pounced and started beating the hell out of me. I was wearing one of those thick duffel coats, the kind Paddington bear wears so the blows had no affect. She pinned me down to the floor, her hand on my right cheek, my head was turned to the left, she was astride me with her weight on my chest giving me a right going over with her right fist. I had my eyes closed in readiness for the fatal blow but when it didn't come and her punches were harmless, I opened them and right in front of my eyes, slightly hidden in the grass, was this beautiful shiny ladies watch with Roman numerals and a lovely red leather strap.

I had never owned a watch before, we couldn't afford things like that. The sight of it filled me with adrenalin, I wanted that watch! From nowhere came this strength, I threw her off me and now it was me on top of her, she curled into a ball and put her hands up to protect her face, but she needn't have bothered, I had no intention of harming her, I got up and left her on the floor as I quickly picked up the watch and legged it home. I would have loved to have seen the look on her face as she saw me running away, probably thinking I was a coward, not knowing I had in my hand my very first watch. I loved that watch even though I had to piece a hole in the strap so it would fit my small wrist. And that was my very first fight, if you can call it that because I didn't really fight back. I have never had a fight since, apart from when a lad on my street wanted my new bike I'd just got for Christmas, I told him it was mine and he couldn't have it, he punched me square in the face and not only knocked me off my bike but knocked me out as well, I woke up to find my bike gone and ran home crying. My big sis got it back though and gave him a good hiding at the same time.

Back on the walk, I tried to persuade Tony to stay until I reached Exmouth but he wouldn't. So next day we took both cars to Swanage which is about 7 miles away from the end of the coast path at Poole. I parked my car up outside Swanage YHA and left a note on the dashboard to let anyone who suspected the car was abandoned know that it wasn't, the note read – WALKING THE SOUTH WEST COAST PATH - I'd like to have added – YOU NOSEY GIT – but I didn't. I thought it would be safe there and I could also stay in the hostel for a night in a couple of week's time if I made it to the end but I wasn't taking anything for granted, it was still a big IF.

I repacked my heavy backpack and Tony, for the last time, dropped me off next day at Kingswear. This time I had two map books with me, the one to Exmouth and the final one to Poole (117 miles) again I was walking towards my car, so if anything bad happened I could just jump in a taxi and pick my car up and go home. Tony and Buddy drove off into the distance leaving me all alone with nothing but a pocket full of money, two sticks and a rucksack, I felt almost naked as I waved goodbye trying not to get emotional. They disappeared around the bend and I put my backpack on, I felt very guilty and selfish for sending Buddy home just so I could complete the walk on my own. But I was now focused on the job in hand. Buddy would be OK, he's spent many a week in Tony's house, this time it would hopefully be only two, he would get a well earned rest and I could concentrate on getting to Poole and fulfilling one of the best achievements of my life.

For the first time, on my own with a heavy bag, I set off, it was a great feeling, that independent feeling returned. The weather had been awful for a week and I know you won't believe me, but the nice weather returned, as soon as Tony turned the corner, the bloody sun came out. It was camping weather once more, how lucky was I?

It took a while to get used to the weight of the bag again, I walked less miles and camped at Brixam at a very basic site with a porta cabin that was the toilet block and a shower that took 50p tokens, the owner was surprised when I asked for two. My shins splints were threatening again, I thought, not now after all these miles! I don't wanna stop now! After two hot showers I limped to the local shops for something for dinner. The man in the caravan next door told me his awning had blown away 2 nights ago causing lots of damage. Thank God I wasn't camping that night.

With my shin splints tightly strapped up I walked towards Torquay next day passing Paignton and Torbay where I sat in the warm October sunshine! Eating ice cream with hordes of other people. The area was too built up to wild camp so I found a cheap B & B next to an off licence and an Indian takeaway, I was in heaven in my room eating curry and drinking lager while watching TV, I'd even had a long soak in a bath, this is definitely the way to do it, this was softing it not roughing it.

After a huge full English breakfast I was off again, I had got lots of supplies from the shop, food and batteries and I topped up my pay as you go phone. I walked under the Oddicombe Cliff Railway, along Babbacombe Bay towards Teignmouth. Peter had given me his itinerary as he didn't need it anymore, he'd written down every name, address and telephone number of every camp site on the way to Poole, another confirmation that he had intended to walk it all. So now I was a little more organised, I phoned ahead and booked a camping spot at the next camp site, I got there and found I was the only camper there, what a waste of time and a phone call that was.

The receptionist told me there was a country and western night in the clubhouse later. I cooked fish fingers and spaghetti on my camp stove, then after showering and doing my laundry I had a choice of going to bed or going to the clubhouse. No way would I normally go listen to country and western but this was different, I wanted a soft seat in a warm room so off I went. I walked to the bar to order a pint of the black stuff, nearly everyone was dressed as either a cowboy or an Indian, I thought Oh My God what have I got myself into. I sat down pretending to read my map book. Then they announced what time the bingo was going to start! Normally I would have walked out but the pint was going down well and the seat was soft so I thought, if you can't beat em' join em' and I bought two bingo tickets so I didn't stand out from the crowd. 8pm came and eyes down, two little ducks quack quack, the game started, I played along for a £30 jackpot, I thought – Is that all? - even if I'd have got a full house there was no way I'd have shouted Bingo, they would have lynched me on the nearest tree!

After bingo the country and western music started, it was live music by a male solo artist with a guitar and computerised backup music. I thought – This is going to be awful – but I was pleasantly surprised when he sounded great and when all the cowboys and Indians got up to dance cowboy style around the dance floor and others started line dancing in the middle, I found myself enjoying my little self so I ordered another pint. They were all very good dancers and it was great to watch. The singer was blind by the way, not that it matters.

The next ferry crossing over the river Teign to Teignmouth runs all year round so I would have no problem catching it and without Buddy I could enjoy the ride and the views for once. It wasn't running, just my luck, due to the recent bad weather, so I had to walk over the road bridge, it was only a mile or two of extra walking, I was clean and my belly was full so I wasn't fussed because today I would reach the end of my third book at Exmouth and would have ONLY 116 miles left to go!

I had to take the inland route from Teignmouth as the tide was too high to take the coastal route so I missed seeing Brunels railway. The going was flat through Dawlish and onto Starcross where I was to catch the ferry that ran until the end of October and would hopefully be running otherwise I would have to swim across the river Exe. It was running and it was nice being able to sit back and enjoy the trip. A man was having the same problem as me with his dog, his dog was howling and barking, it hated the reverse thrust, the poor man, I didn't envy him.

I headed for the nearest camp sites about two miles down the path, there were two marked on my map so no worries! There was only one and it wasn't a camp site but the biggest holiday park I have ever seen, it was bigger than the town I live in, it even had it's own Burger King! Miles upon miles of static vans, it took me 20 minutes and a mile walking just to get to the reception. They told me they didn't allow camping and I couldn't use their facilities either, basically they said bugger off. So I buggered off and wild camped in a secluded spot around the corner and sneaked in later to use their shop for food and lovely beer.

I walked through the giant site next day back to the path hoping I could use their toilet but the only toilet block I could find was closed for the season. I walked cross legged for an hour or two until I found one at Budleigh Salterton . Oh what a relief! I found a post office at the back of the Co Op where at great expense I posted my third map book home, three down one to go. I replenished my rations and filled my belly with food and fruit. I passed a butchers where feathered dead ducks hanging by their necks were on display outside, it's not often I see this sort of thing, I've only ever seen them paddling about on ponds.

That night I had my second wild camp on the run, it was just past Sidmouth, the going had got tough again, steep up and downs, the weather was still warm, I couldn't believe it, it was October! I camped right next to the sea about a foot off the beach it was a lovely spot but a bit frightening as it was very close to the sea edge. I hoped I had judged the high tide correctly, I didn't want the sea to join me in my sleeping bag, if I'd got it wrong I'd be floating. It was by a river so I had water but I won't say where it was because no one in their right mind would camp there. I tried to inflate my sleeping mat but to my horror found that I must have punctured it on a thorn bush as I walked. I spent most of the night trying to blow it up but gave up and had an uncomfortable nights sleep.

With aching hips and back, I continued onto Beer next day, what a great name, then onto Seaton. I was on a mission to find a puncture repair kit for my mat. I couldn't get hold of one so I bought a cheap foam mat and tied it to my pack. I trudged on through the endless woods into Lyme Regis where I arrived not only knackered but three day old smelly, in dire need of a shower again I made the biggest cock up yet!

The tourist information centre in Lyme Regis (or Lyme to the locals) was shut but a kind elderly couple in the museum assured me that Hook Farm was open for tents and gave me directions – now I either didn't hear them correctly or they gave me the wrong directions because I got totally lost. It's horrible being lost when you are knackered, smelly, walking in circles and nearly in tears. I saw a man wheeling his green bins out, I was desperate so I asked him would he give me a lift. What a lovely gent because he not only said yes but said he knew a better site where his wife went swimming. I phoned this site up to make sure they were open, they were but the office closed in 10 minutes. The guy flung my heavy bag in the back of his car and I quickly jumped in, thankful that he was getting me out of a hole. We sped off and arrived at Wood Farm camp site two minutes later. I thanked him and waved goodbye, he drove off and as soon as he did I realised I didn't have my phone with me, I must have dropped it, I was gutted as my Dad had bought it for my birthday and it had all the photos of the walk and all my contacts in it. Bugger!

I booked in at the office before they closed and explained what just happened. They looked at me like I was a lunatic as I told them a stranger had given me a lift and I'd left my phone in his car, I had no idea who he was or where he lived. Here was a mad woman who stank and looked like a tramp who took lifts from strangers who was now asking for another so she could go get her phone back. They flatly denied me any assistance because they were closing up and counting the takings, I didn't blame them, it was my own fault for getting in such a pickle, they did ring my phone but no one answered, was it lying near the bins or in his car?

I was almost in tears, what should I do? The only thing I could think of was to ask someone in one of the caravans for a lift, they all had cars parked outside. The first one thought I was a nutter when I explained and closed the door in my face. The second turned out to be one of the nicest gentleman I will ever meet, his name was John Bradley, he was sat writing a book about caravanning ("Eighty Years of Enjoying Caravanning"). He was in his nineties and had been caravanning for 80 years thus the book title. He listened to my story and didn't hesitate to give me a lift back to the bins where hopefully I would find the man and my phone. We did find it and in the mans car, in the foot well, there it was, one missed call, he said he was a bit deaf and didn't hear it ringing. So John took me back to his caravan, in his brand new Bentley, I was sat there stinking, he was too much of a gent to say anything, his wife had kindly minded my bag. If I wasn't so smelly I would have give him a kiss on the cheek but his wife looked on and his dinner was waiting on the table. John was my knight in shining armour, I am going to buy a copy of his book and I hope he reads this one some day. Cheers John, you are one of the last true gentlemen of this world.

I put my tent up in the dark and managed to calm down in the luxurious bath that I found in the shower block, the site was very clean and tidy, I'd like to go back one day.

Because I'd got a lift, I'd missed about two miles of the coast path. I walked there and back next day while my tent dried, I had walked every inch of the path up to now and wasn't going to cheat now. I then packed up and continued towards charming Charmouth then over Golden Cap. This walk seemed to be taking a lifetime. Thinking of the first couple of weeks as I walked along, it seemed years ago not weeks that I had started in Minehead, so I told myself to not think about it. It made me a little stressed but who would have thought it at the start, I had no intention of walking all 630 miles and here I was going for the finish like some demented sprinter with her legs tied together - would I get home in time to start my Christmas shopping or before it started snowing? I definitely wanted to be home before November 5th and bonfire night, what with all these cock ups and wasted time and miles it was taking for ever, so I made myself think of anything but the finish at Poole.

At the pub in Seatown I treated myself to some lunch, salad and chips, salad for the nutrition and chips for the calories. A woman on the next table ordered a crab sandwich which looked delicious but expensive, her husband ordered a ploughman's lunch, I noticed she ate hers and then kept pinching bits of his cheese, he didn't seem to mind, isn't love wonderful.

I decided to pack in early and camped at West Bay camp site. And that's where I met him.....

CHAPTER 11
Would I Get Home Before Christmas?

John Wright (names have been changed to protect the innocent) is an ex soldier and survival expert, or that's what he told me as I put my tent up next to his. The sun was still warm and we talked and talked and talked while we were sat down on the grass. I liked him straight away even though he told me he was 67 years old, he didn't look it, he was wearing a tightly fitted ' Help For Heroes ' tee shirt and I could see he was very fit for his age. He talked with a very posh accent which is amazing because I found out later that he was born in Oldham which is just up the road from where I live. He didn't say path or bath, he said parth and barth. We got on well and ended up eating together at the camp sites restaurant, but not before I had found a bath in the toilet block, not only to have a lovely soak but I also used it to locate the miniature hole in my self inflating sleeping mat. Just like fixing a puncture in a bicycle tube, I found the hole and fixed it using the only thing I had available - a compeed plaster, it worked a treat.

John had also, like that other guy I'd met, ' bombed ' it from Minehead and was trying to get to Poole in 4 weeks, but when he found he couldn't, he slowed down and would settle for 6 weeks. I found I wanted to be totally honest with him and admitted that I had been walking for over 7 weeks already but explained I had set off at my own pace not knowing I would walk it all, and if I would have rushed it, like most people do, I would probably have injured myself and not got as far. He told me an old war wound in his hip was playing up and he would have to take it easy.

He was walking the path for the charity 'Help For Heroes' and was to raise about 6 grand. It never occurred to me to walk for charity because I never intended to do the whole thing. If I had started with the aim of walking 630 miles, I may have considered it but then that's a whole new ball game. If you commit yourself to a charity you are more under pressure to succeed and I wouldn't have liked that. I probably would have failed anyway, as it was, I was still going even if it was taking me forever.

In the morning, I gave him a fiver for his charity thinking he would walk off at a heady pace and I would never see him again but he didn't, we walked together and chatted and chatted, you get my drift, we talked each others socks down. I suppose we were both in dire need of some company. We walked together, he slowed his pace a little for me and I only very slightly quickened up a bit for him. His bag weighed a ton, I won't go into why because he's writing his own book, he can tell the tale himself.

John wanted to go to Abbotsbury and stay in a B & B, I wanted to camp to save money, the weather, considering the time of year was still fantastic, I think I convinced him to camp for that reason, he agreed and we camped at a site called Bagwith Farm that had a brand new toilet block with several baths in that took 50p coins. So after we cleared the shop of food and wine and we'd sat in his tent eating and drinking, we both went for a bath to warm up. The evening temperature was noticeably cooler now as the month wore on, it was now the 12th of October. Would I get home before Christmas?

I made a cup of tea for John in the morning and we both set off heading for the Island of Portland. I voiced my concerns about Lulworth Army Ranges which were further up the path and were only open at weekends and sometimes not even then. He told me not to worry about it, but I was worried, it would take an enormous inland detour to get around these ranges if they were shut when we got there. So when we got to Chesil Beach and had lovely omelettes for lunch in a pub, I phoned the ranges up and found out they were open the next weekend from 10am, we both sat and worked out that we could get there in time. "Great!" John said he was pleased and could I now shut up about it. It's a good job I liked him.

There are no camp sites on Portland so we knew we would have to wild camp. At Portland Bill which is at the end of the island, we shared a cream tea in the cafe, the owner ripped up the bill when he found out John was walking for charity. I won't say where we camped that night but it wasn't far from the pub where we had steak and chips and a lot of beer, well I did, John said he wasn't much of a drinker.

Next day we walked up the other side of the island to Weymouth. We were getting on like a house on fire and the miles just slipped on by. I started to just follow him like a lost sheep and stopped reading my map, we went wrong for a few miles and had to retrace our steps but I didn't mind a bit, I really liked him. We had walked around the island and decided to have another omelette in the same pub as they were so delicious.

At Weymouth the ferry had stopped running for the season but it was only a short walk over the bridge and into town were I stocked up on supplies. We carried on and went looking for a camp site at Bowleaze Cove. The first one didn't take tents much to the annoyance of John, I thought, I am glad it's not just me this happens to. We were directed to another which was more like a Butlins camp with entertainment and swimming pools, it was packed. We both did some laundry, two backpackers getting cleaned up for a change not just me on me own, both on the same mission, to get to Poole. We ate in the restaurant, had beer and played pool, John beat me, or did I let him win?

It was Friday when we set off next day towards Osmington Mills, we past the Smugglers Inn which I'd like to frequent one day. Still talking each others socks down, John telling me tales of his army days which I can't repeat because he swore me to secrecy, we laughed as we passed a sign
for a place called ' Scratchy Bottom ' honestly who comes up with these names?

Tomorrow the ranges would be open so we camped at Newlands Farm overlooking the beautiful view of Durdle Door, a natural rock arch jutting out to sea. John got a £50 donation from the owners, which was very kind of them. We ate in the bar and had a few pints again, this was all very jolly and having someone with me

103

was making the going easier and a little more enjoyable. We talked about how we might feel when we reached the end. There were only a few pages left in my map book, I was now beginning to believe I would definitely make it now even if I had to crawl on hands and knees to Poole.

It took all day to get through the ranges, it was hard going, lots of up and downs, the weather was still fantastic, the air was clear as glass. I regretted not having a better camera as the views were stunning especially around Lulworth Cove. I took some photos with my phone not knowing the settings were wrong and it was taking pictures the size of a stamp, I didn't find out until I got home, never mind it's a good excuse to do the whole 630 mile walk again. (NOT!)

We got through the ranges and it was time to camp, there was nothing marked on our maps apart from one inland at a place called Smedmore. John didn't want to wild camp, he said he hadn't wild camped at all on the path, he said he liked a bit of comfort which surprised me as he was an ex survival expert, but you know what they say about experts, they are a drip under pressure, but there is another saying "Any fool can be uncomfortable". So we had to walk inland looking for this site and when we got there we found it was one of those bloody Caravan Club sites that don't allow campers. This snotty fat git came over and told us in no uncertain terms to get out, John got a bit annoyed and I could see his fists clenching but he managed to keep his temper. A young couple saw us walking off with our tails between our legs and invited us in their mobile home for tea and biscuits. They were a lovely couple and even gave us some of their milk to take with us. The sun was a half hour away from setting as we trudged back to where we left the coast path, we had no choice but to set up camp illegally near a toilet block. We waited until it got dark so no one could see us before we put the tents up and while we waited we sat down and made something to eat. John had run out of things to eat and there were no shops nearby, all he had was a strawberry milk drink, the stuff that dieters take when trying to lose weight, so we shared my rations of noodles and custard, the stuff I'd been eating all along the walk. I didn't mind giving him my precious food because I liked him and I knew we'd be in some sort of civilisation tomorrow and wouldn't need it. He said how nice the food was but we were both starving so an old boot would have tasted nice at that time.

We were both knackered and got in our tents, I put my ipod on and listened to music and was asleep about two seconds later so I didn't hear my tent being violently shaken an hour later by a man shouting ' You in there - Get out '. John heard it though, and when the man got no response from me he started shaking John's tent. John got out and the guy shouted at him and asked him had he not seen the "no camping" signs, John said he hadn't, which was true as there weren't any. John explained, very calmly that we had walked through the firing ranges and were walking the coast path for charity, this seemed to calm the guy down and they ended up chatting, the guy said he was the warden and had trouble with gangs of youths camping here but it was OK on this occasion for us to stay so long as we were gone by 9am.

I was oblivious to all this, it had been one of my worst nightmares, me wild camping on my own, some man would come, shaking my tent, shouting for me to get out in the middle of the night, if this would have happened when I was on my own, I would have been very scared!

John was there thank God and dealt with the situation, good on him. He told me all about it in the morning as we drank some hot strawberry drink for breakfast (yuk). The ground and tents were white with frost, it was the first time the temperature had dropped below freezing, it was definitely time to get home.

We hadn't had a decent meal for two days and were hungry, as the sun came up so did the temperature, we walked on towards Swanage. By the afternoon it was really warm and we came across a group having a picnic, sat in the sun, (on the 17th October!) When we told them what we were doing, they gave us biscuits and fruit and congratulated us on completing such a long walk. We were still shocked at how generous people were with food and kindness, this time we were both very humbled, they even gave John some money for his charity. I regretted now not doing it for charity, I witnessed on many occasions John receiving donations along the way, people were great about it and had no hesitation in donating, I witnessed the joy of the giver and the receiver.

We approached Swanage, 7 miles away from the end. We decided we would spoil ourselves and book into a B & B and have a proper dinner to celebrate. I'd only stayed in two up to now which had saved me a fortune, not like the couple who were walking from John O'Groats to Land's End and had booked 95 consecutive Bed and Breakfasts in advance all that forward planning! I wonder if they made it, I would love to know.

At Swanage we found a B & B. I had an en-suite room, how very posh, and wallowed in its luxury and softness, I had a bath and then a shower just because I could. Later, on the way to dinner, I checked on my car which was still there outside the YHA. We ate in an expensive Italian restaurant, I chose the cheapest option and it was delicious, not a bloody noodle in sight! We went into a pub after and I ordered a pint of the black stuff, John wasn't impressed with how much I drank I could tell, he said he would never get used to seeing a woman drinking from a pint glass, well he is fifteen years older than me and from a different generation where men were men and women knew about it!

CHAPTER 12
A Bigger Bolder Adventure

So this was the last day, only seven miles to go to South Haven and the end of our 630 mile journey. The owners of the B & B packed us a lovely picnic lunch for free which was very kind of them. We set off yapping away as usual, we walked past the famous chalk stacks of Old Harry and his wife and after all this time we still managed to go wrong and ended up off the path and in a small wooded valley. We heard a loud cry that was a cross between a cow and an elephant, we looked up to see a large deer stag with huge antlers. It stared at us with disgust, we were on his patch, it then ran off into the trees.

And that was the last memory I have of my walk before we eventually and thankfully reached the blue metal sculpture that marks the end of the South West Coast Path. This was it then! It was over. No fanfares, no fireworks, no one there to congratulate us. We took some pictures then John started walking away, I tapped him on the shoulder and said "Hey John, Congratulations, Well Done". He congratulated me and we shook hands, we both knew what we had achieved, we didn't really need anybody to tell us.

John's friend arrived to pick him up and I caught the open topped bus back into Swanage and my car. I waved goodbye and blew him a kiss from the top deck as he drove past. I sat there, on the bus, wind blowing through my hair, moving without moving my legs, it was a weird sensation. I felt very very proud of myself, what an achievement! It had taken me 64 days to do the walk, twice as many as some people take but it didn't matter. I had walked the whole path and had not missed out an inch of it. I drove home and was back by 11pm.

It is now two weeks later, it's November and winter is nearly upon us, the clocks have been turned back and dark evenings are here again. I made it back before the snow. I am sat in my caravan writing this book, I have loved writing it as it's been like walking the path all over again, reminiscing about the good and bad times. I miss the kindness that people showed me along the way and the lovely weather I was lucky enough to have. If it had been bad weather I know I wouldn't have made it. Most of all I miss the independence and total freedom I felt that came with being self sufficient, not a lot of women in this world can experience that feeling. The walk has filled me with confidence and self belief.

I know I haven't written much about the scenery or the sights and sounds I saw and heard along the way or the beautiful views and the fantastic things I witnessed as I walked this 630 mile path. If I were to describe everything in detail, this book would be the size of War and Peace. All I would like to say is if you ever get the chance, for a day, a week, a month or more, try walking on the path yourself, I guarantee, if you get decent weather, you will not be disappointed. Walking this path was physically and mentally difficult, you have to be slightly insane to attempt to backpack it all in one go but I have to say, it is one of the best things I have ever done.

Last weekend I met up with John, he was visiting his sister and was collecting some of his sponsorship money. We both said we missed the lifestyle of backpacking and we talked about how lucky we were with the weather on the walk. We both said we were still knackered and our feet hurt when we stood on them, we both couldn't stop eating and we were finding it hard to sleep in our comfortable beds. But we had recovered enough to talk of a bigger, bolder adventure, a walk not of 630 miles but one of 5000 miles. Not Land's End to John O'Groats but John O'Groats to John O'Groats - A walk that would take not 8 weeks but 12 months. Next year we plan to walk around the coast of mainland Britain.

CPSIA information can be obtained at www.ICGtesting.com
Printed in the USA
LVOW072111091012

302156LV00022B/12/P